Kevin Mullin enlisted in the British Army aged fifteen years and eight months. He served in several conflict areas and operations around the globe, then at the age of thirty-four, he left the service and became a private military operator. Kevin was contracted to the United States Department of Defense, securing and protecting US Military bases and assets in Afghanistan. Kevin worked there for four years before moving to one of the most valuable targets in Afghanistan in the heart of Kabul – The Serena Hotel. Kevin studied NLP within the British Army and gained a wealth of knowledge and experience, training the trainers in the methods of approaches to NLP. Having suffered the loss of both his brother and mother, he was crippled with anxiety for many years. Kevin searched relentlessly for new, dynamic ways to beat it.

Having taken an apprenticeship with Ali Campbell, Kevin finally found what he was looking for. He understudied and role modelled Ali to great effect. In June 2017, Kevin opened his very own NLP practice based in Central Scotland. The practice has received rave reviews about Kevin's new, dynamic and direct approach. He has helped thousands of clients become anxiety-free. Kevin has gained plaudits from Italy, Dubai and America for his dynamic and enthusiastic approach to motivational speaking and helping businesses and organisations flourish and grow. He is also a full-time parent. He raises his children with the approach he takes in life and in his crusade to help everyone in the battle with anxiety. Drive, determination and a vigour unparalleled in this modern age.

Dedicated to the loving memory of my wee mammy, Kathleen Mullin, who, in the end, just couldn't beat her anxiety. But you can.

Kevin Mullin

ANXIETY, IT'S TIME TO GO

AUSTIN MACAULEY PUBLISHERS™

LONDON • CAMBRIDGE • NEW YORK • SHARJAH

A CIP catalogue record for this title is available from the British Library.

ISBN 9781528929745 (Paperback)
ISBN 9781528929752 (Hardback)
ISBN 9781528929769 (E-Book)

www.austinmacauley.com

First Published (2019)
Austin Macauley Publishers Ltd
25 Canada Square
Canary Wharf
London
E14 5LQ

Everything in life happens for a reason, exactly the same as the sun rising in the morning and setting in the evening. This was the case when I stumbled upon NLP in 2005 whilst serving in the British Army. The journey has been chaotic at times. It has been crazy and even beautiful, with so many people having a direct influence on this book. I don't have enough pages to thank everyone, so if I miss anyone out, please accept my apologies. Without these people, I wouldn't have a book to write.

Dr Richard Bandler and John Grinder, for creating NLP and making the work I do possible. Dr Bandler's influence helped sculpt NLP. These fast, effective methods and techniques have changed millions of people's lives.

Mr Ali Campbell, for re-defining how NLP is taught and practiced; for his streamlined, no-nonsense approach which I have embraced in every way. I will be forever grateful to him for seeing potential in me and planting the seed of fast, effective change. My thanks also for stepping in when needed and guiding me to this destination.

My spiritual advisor, Ms Angela Cowan, for her work and her guidance on the spiritual side of the book. I would have faltered without her. Her energy shines like a bright star and positivity radiates from her soul.

Mr Steven Wark and Mr Allan Stubbs, both former British Army soldiers. They installed in me the pride, passion and drive I wake up with every day.

And finally, to my beautiful children, who inspire me to be the very best person I can. They have always been by my side and always will be.

Table of Contents

Why NLP?

There are many different therapies and ways of doing business out there. The question you may ask first is, "Why NLP?" For me to give you that answer, I need to explain what NLP is and how quickly it works. With so many explanations for what NLP is and what it does, it is best described with this small tale.

Three generations of the same family all live in one house. The grandparent is eighty years old, the parent is forty years old, and the next in line is twenty years old. The parent is an NLP practitioner with his own practice, and the child wants to know what it is. The young adult approaches the parent and asks what exactly NLP is, and the parent replies:

"I will teach you and tell you and even show you what NLP is, so you get it straight away, but first I need you to do me a favour."

"OK, no problem."

"See your grandparent over there? Go ask them how they are feeling today and what they think about the weather."

So the young adult says to the grandparent, "How are you feeling today and what about this awful weather?"

"Oh, not good," the grandparent replies in a deep voice, looking down at his trembling hands. "You know this weather makes my bones cold and it affects me something awful and I shake from head to toe."

The young adult then says to the parent, "Did you hear that?"

"Yes," the parent replied. "Now go back over and ask them about the happiest day of their entire life, what it was and do they still remember it?"

Off the young adult goes again and asks, "Out of interest, what was the happiest day of your life and can you remember it?"

Immediately, the grandparent sits bolt upright in the chair. With a huge smile, he starts to talk about the birth of his first child. He describes how he remembers it and how much love he felt. As he speaks, he uses his hands to express joy, with no shaking.

"Did you hear that?" said the young adult.

The parent replied, "Yes I did, and that is NLP in its purest of forms. You changed the emotional state and thinking patterns. You used words, leading to new thoughts, leading to emotions and then actions. That is Neuro Linguistic Programming."

Neuro = How the mind operates.

Linguistics = The language we use and how it affects us.

Programming = How we sequence actions to do what we want.

One of the best explanations I have read is by a gentleman called Robert Dilts[1] and his explanation of NLP is:

"NLP is whatever works."

And that's why I choose NLP – that one statement. It says, don't be afraid to try new, different and unknown methods and techniques. Play around with them, tweak, twist and turn them to suit your needs, wants and desires. Use everything you have to get to the end state, and for me that sums NLP. Life is full of rules with no rules if you will. A sequence of words, thoughts and emotions leads us to the end state. This particular end state is to be anxiety-free.

NLP was formed in the 1970s by two gentlemen. One was a professor and one a student. They researched and studied human behaviour. They wanted to see why some people excelled at certain things and some didn't. Fascinated by this, they developed theories which became the foundations for early NLP.

The gentleman was Professor John Grinder and the student was Richard Bandler. They created one of the most effective and fast-acting therapies out there to date, NLP. NLP has come a long way since its birth in the '70s. Like every newborn, it grows and learns, and continues to grow until it has matured. Over the past forty or so years, it has grown to what we have now.

NLP has a set of principles to work within and also presuppositions. These are the basic guiding directions which allow you to use it to its most effective state. NLP is all about fixing you, so that later, if you need to, you can fix others along the way. There would be no point fixing everyone else and leaving yourself to the last. NLP allows you to put yourself first and become the person you want and know you can be.

The Pillars of NLP are as follows[2]:

1. You – your emotional state and level of skill.
2. The presuppositions – the principles of NLP.
3. Rapport – the quality of relationships.
4. Outcome – knowing what you want.
5. Feedback – how will you know you are getting what you want?
6. Flexibility – if what you are doing isn't getting results, change the method.

The reason I have listed and described these is that as the book goes on, you will be able to see and identify each one. In turn, this allows you to understand NLP that little bit more with each part. This book isn't about teaching you NLP. I am not going to list the thirteen presuppositions in turn. But I am going to list the ones which are relevant for you later on. These statements may seem strange at first. You may not believe them to begin with, but bear with me, as by the end of the book, every single one will make perfect sense[2].

People respond to experience, not reality itself. People make the best choice they can at the time. All actions have purpose.

Every behaviour has a positive intention (pay close attention to this one).

We already have all the resources we need, or we can create them. We process all information through our senses.

If you want to understand, act.

These are a few of the presuppositions of NLP, the ones which will make perfect sense to you as you progress. A good idea at this point is to keep a pen handy as you read the book. At the end of each chapter, come back to this page and tick off the ones you learn during the chapter. You will soon discover how quickly they are all ticked off.

Some of the leading therapists in the world are NLP practitioners who use these methods. Media hypnotist Paul McKenna. Celebrity life coach Ali Campbell. Derren Brown. NLP is changing the way therapy is conducted. The more people learn and discover it, the more popular it becomes. Some of the

A-list clients who have had NLP therapy say it all: Cheryl Cole, Katie Price and Kelly Rowlands, to name a few. The late darts player Eric Bristow. Every sports team has an NLP practitioner on board. This increases confidence, drive and determination.

So it was an easy choice to use NLP-based methods and techniques to get you to change your life. Everyone whose life it touches, changes. It can be very quick and has the longevity element ingrained.

Preface

"Anxiety is an emotion characterised by feelings of tension, worried thoughts and physical changes like increased blood pressure. People with anxiety disorders usually have recurring intrusive thoughts or concerns. They may avoid certain situations out of worry, concern or fear."

So there you have it: the definitive definition of anxiety as per the wisdom of Wikipedia.

To most people, it's just a bunch of words someone came up with to describe the fear and emotions which eat at you every day if you suffer from it. What it doesn't state is that like any emotion, thought or feeling, it can be replaced as easily as it was created. How do you manage that? Well, that's the best part. YOU – yes, you – already have everything you need to defeat this crippling emotion. This thought process controls your day-to-day living, affects your overall mood, and isolates you from friends, family, work and relationships. In fact, if anxiety had its way, you would be nothing more than a recluse who stayed indoors and didn't challenge or test yourself in any way, shape or form. It would happily keep you as confused as the day you were born.

What we sometimes fail to understand is that emotions are normal. Even the negative ones and in particular, anxiety. Without them, you wouldn't push yourself to your limits, start projects or undertake any real sort of challenge in life. Anxiety is an emotion which can be used to achieve greatness in all areas of your personal and professional life. This book will help you understand and learn that anxiety can be controlled and even utilised to your advantage. It will teach you how to gain control of your life and propel yourself forward instead of taking a back seat.

Many people want to change and take back control. They want to be free from the one emotion which sits dominantly on top of all others. But not many people take action, and here's the first great part of this book – it acknowledges you and your action. You have made the first step, you are looking for answers, and by buying and reading this book it shows how hungry you are for the answers you haven't been given so far.

What is anxiety, and how do I beat it?

For that, I say, "Well done."

You have started a journey to discover, learn and beat the crippling emotion called anxiety. Someone once told me in my previous career in the British Army that pain is weakness leaving the body. Well, having severe and crippling anxiety after leaving the service, I was soon to discover that pain is not weakness leaving the body. It is exactly what it says – pain. No words of encouragement or understanding or even tough love will make it any less painful or easier to understand.

Emotional pain can be just as debilitating as physical pain. Sometimes physical pain is much easier to deal with. Bones heal, cuts and bruises go away, and you recover much quicker at times from these. Emotional pain can't be judged or seen from the outside. More often than not it lasts a great deal longer. So instead of suffering in silence, wouldn't it be good if you all knew a way to treat and deal with the emotional pain you face? That's what this book will show you. It will let you understand what happened. Why it happened? And the most important part: how to start the self-healing process. We are going to do this using some direct and forward-thinking Neuro Linguistics Programming. It will give you much more than knowledge: it will give you the tools you need to really let go.

In the battle to overcome anxiety, one of the key tools is knowledge. No one sits down and takes the time to explain why this emotion is dominant over all others. It can control your life and your way of thinking. That usually puts the body into flight mode. You try to avoid the reality and when you can't get away from it or understand it, you spiral into a negative mind set, this is me and it isn't going to go away.

With more knowledge comes more power. More power increases your desire to beat it. When you have that desire, you can go at it full-on each day until it is gone. Anxiety is nothing more than an emotion. It's not a crippling illness. It's not a disease. It's not inherent in your DNA. It is an emotion with negative side effects which sprout like branches on a tree. What starts as something small and minor can quickly spiral out of control. It cuts us off from family, friends, partners and even children.

Anxiety is one of the most misunderstood emotions. It's often looked on as a lifestyle to those who suffer from it. People try different ways to cope and get through the day. They try different breathing, positive thought patterns and isolation to dull it, but it just never goes away. Sufferers wake with that heavy, dark, sombre feeling – the first thing you notice before you even open your eyes. Having been there myself, I wish I'd discovered the knowledge and techniques in this book during my battle.

The good news is, you have what I missed back then.

This book will give you knowledge about anxiety and the tools to beat it. What you have now is a kick-start to your recovery. So you begin. You read and practise. You re-read and you practise again. And you never, ever give in.

Everyone is capable of beating anxiety and its side effects. Everyone is capable of an anxiety-free lifestyle.

This book will show you how. Together we can beat it.

1

Where It All Began

Every journey has a beginning, and I think by sharing it will let you see that this book is based on fact. It's written by someone who knew anxiety only too well. At some stages in my life, it was my only companion in the world. A very destructive and negative companion, but at one point a few years back, it was all I had to hold onto. Anxiety was a badge I wore to excuse my behaviours, thoughts and emotions. At the time, it was something which gave me an excuse to simply give in.

I was born in Irvine, Scotland, on the 21st of February 1976, the youngest of three children. I grew up in a normal family environment until the age of nine, when my father left the family home. I was left to deal with the consequences, along with my older brother Alan. Nothing was going to be easy from that moment onwards. But everything happened for a reason and I soon learned to look at every event as a lesson. I took what I needed from it in order to make it in the world.

I grew up with an alcoholic mother and no father. Life was hard from the get-go and it wouldn't be kind for many years. The battles I faced in my personal life and in my military career would eventually develop a survival instinct. This saved me when anxiety came calling with force and wouldn't go away.

On January 1992, aged fifteen years and ten months, I enlisted in the Royal Green Jackets, one of the finest Infantry foot regiments the British army created. These guys were a London-based regiment. No Scots enlisted apart from my brother Alan and another young man from Glasgow called Steve. From that day onwards, and for the next seventeen years of my life, I would be known as Jock. No one cared for first names, and even if they did, they wouldn't have heard me speak. It was hard from the start. All the instructors, the staff, and the lads were from

London, Liverpool, Cornwall and Newcastle. I was standing out. I could have chosen to join my local Scottish infantry regiment, but where was the fun in that? I would just be another guy from another small town in Scotland, like the rest of them. For some reason, I didn't want that. I wanted to stand out. I wanted to be pushed harder than the others, and I must say, they didn't disappoint.

On the 21st of December 1992, I completed my military training and became Rifleman Kevin Mullin. Because I was still sixteen and too young to serve, I couldn't join my unit in Northern Ireland. I was kept behind with the other under-age guys and put on a machine gun course for six months. I remember being disappointed at first, but when the course kicked in, the days became harder and faster than before. So, I started to enjoy life as a GPMG machine gunner.

When that was over, I took my first posting to Northern Ireland. The ceasefire hadn't been called yet, so it was still full-on. Again, being just short of eighteen, I was put in the kitchens to help clean pots and pans and do general duties. Unhappy with army life, I remember my brother coming to me and saying, "Remember, just push on; don't make waves and keep your mouth shut. Soon you'll be eighteen and on patrol."

Eighteen came and I went on patrol. Not one sign of anxiety showed itself. Fear, excitement, and intimidation, yes. But no anxiety. Not yet, anyway. I knew the second I stepped out of a small operating base called Rockwood that this was the life for me. From there, I was deployed to: Northern Ireland, Cyprus, Egypt, Jordan, Bosnia, Kosovo, Falkland Isles, Canada, Kenya and Iraq.

I rose through the ranks and gained the prestige title of Warrant Officer Class II. At this point, my life completely changed. I was introduced to NLP. Things happen for a reason. I guess I was just in the right place at the right time on this occasion, walking down the corridor in the Infantry Battle School. I heard a shout from the officer commanding my division asking who was outside. After stating, "Warrant Officer Mullin," I heard, "ah, just the very man I was looking for. In you come and park your arse."

They have such a delicate way of making their intentions clear…

I was told that the British army was sending someone to Bangor University in North Wales for four to six months, to study NLP with the international sports performance and enhancement professor. I was the person in his line of sight when he got the call, so that person would be me. I remember thinking, *What is NLP?* I hadn't finished secondary school and could barely read or write when I joined the army. But it was happening. I would go and study NLP.

The problem the British Army faced at the time was a high fail rate on the combat infantry course. This was due to the rigours and demands on the body, but also the mind. They wanted to re-look at how the British Army instructors trained and how they projected themselves onto the students. The old adage of 'do as I say and not as I do' simply wasn't working at the time. My entire world opened up: I finished the study and gained a diploma in NLP, then returned for the task of training the trainers. The army wanted to get the best out of students and staff alike using the fundamentals I learned on the course.

From that moment on, I was hooked.

I would spend every day developing, re-framing, and watching for cues and people's sub modalities. It was a whole new world. I submerged myself deep within it. I knew there and then that this was something I wanted to do, and if I ever did leave the British Army, this would be my calling.

Life has a funny way of never throwing anything at you that you can't handle. Around the end of this stage, my marriage broke up and I separated from the mother of my two beautiful girls. I can't recall much from that time, but it was more heartbreak than anxiety washing over me day by day. At times you become confused about the emotions you face, and it's easy to blame everything on one thing if it gives you a reason to justify your behaviour. For me, I was simply heartbroken for the first time in my life.

One of my gifts I hold above everything is my children. I adore being a father. When custody was awarded to the girls' mother, I was crushed. I had been conditioned for so many years to just get on with it, so I fell into that trap. I resigned my position in the British Army. Then I took a job with a private security company, as a private contractor for the United States Department of Defence. My thinking at the time was like most people: *if I don't face reality, then it isn't happening.* I had also lost my brother. It was one of the worst years I can recall. So it was decided that I would live and work in Afghanistan and come back home every three months to see the girls. Privately, I decided that I would only ever return to live in the UK if I had my girls back.

By writing this book and running my therapy and coaching practice, that dream became a reality. After seven long years in some of the worst locations and situations, I have ever encountered, I had a home in the UK and my girls with me. The point of the story is: never give up on hope and your dreams. No matter how long they take, they can become a reality. I will say wholeheartedly that the journey from the end of my military service was – for want of a better word – brutal. Up until a year ago when I stumbled upon a gentleman called Ali Campbell.

For anyone who knows anything about NLP and coaching, his name will sound very familiar. This gentleman opened up my world to a whole new way of thinking, acting and believing. He re-educated me in the ways of NLP and totally streamlined it to the fast effect change mode I work with now. He is my redemption in life; a light that shone so bright I simply had no choice but to follow it. That's when everything fell into place and I finally realised my calling in life. I knew where my passion lay, and exactly how to utilise it and make the same change in others that I made in myself.

For that, I will be eternally grateful.

The whole fast effective change model works, and it works so much better than anyone believes. Some views are, there's no such thing as a quick fix. I remember sitting in an interview with a national media outlet and the reporter asked was there such a thing as a quick fix. My friend and mentor Ali Campbell replied to the question without hesitation and it's the very same answer I give today when asked the same question: so there is a long fix? If both outlooks and approaches achieve the very same outcome, then surely it is better to do it quickly and effectively as opposed to the long drawn out version. As long as the change happens in a safe, secure manner, and it has the longevity element to it, then I say quick fix each and every time.

I lived the first thirty years of my life anxiety-free, so I was naive to the whole emotion. I knew it existed. I heard people talk about it. I knew it was a real emotion but I never understood it. Reading all the books in the world and listening to people talk about it for hours on end, gives you knowledge but it doesn't give you understanding. When it comes to beating anxiety, the person helping you beat it needs an understanding of it and not from just books, papers or lectures.

Knowledge and understanding are two different elements. I have knowledge of anxiety. I studied for months and years on the subject. But what makes this so effective is that I have a deep understanding of it also. My understanding is greater than I could ever have imagined when I set out on this journey we call life.

I know that huge, heavy feeling that strikes at your very core the second you open your eyes in the morning. I know the agitation that consumes you at a moment's notice. The anxiety and panic attacks which wash over you like a tsunami and don't let go. The not wanting to get out of bed each morning and the overall feeling of dullness that consumes your entire day, week, month, and – in some cases – years.

In this book, I am going to tell you, but also show you how to regain the control and understanding you need to free yourself from this all-consuming emotion. I am going to give you what is needed to rise above it like a titan and walk down an anxiety-free road.

Before you get started again, I just want to say to each and every one of you reading this book:

BLOODY WELL DONE!

You have the instincts to beat it. You have the desire to know more. And shortly you will have the tools you need to take you where you want to be. The key here is actions not words. Happiness and change comes through action. You can sit all day and talk at a conscious level, but it won't make a difference. The thing eating away at you sits at a subconscious level, so for change to happen it needs to be there.

So let's get started and make that change you have wanted and searched for.

2

My First Taste of Anxiety

I remember it like it was yesterday, and if I really focus on the intensity I could certainly re-live it. Anxiety was something I hadn't felt before. And what triggered it? My fifty-two-year-old mother was diagnosed with terminal cancer. That was the start of my relationship with anxiety.

I was in the city Ghazni in Afghanistan at the time and it wasn't the best of places. I received a phone call from my mum – an unheard-of occurrence – and I knew this was serious. I remember her words. She asked when I would be home, and I said I had around five weeks to go before I was back. She said I needed to come and see her when I returned, as she was not very well and needed to talk to me.

I asked a million questions and all she said was, "It's OK, son; it's nothing serious, but you need to come here." She asked me to promise that I would come, so of course I promised. My mum was a fighter and never let anything stand in her way. The fact that she needed to see me as soon as I got home had me overthinking, and then I entered the whole catastrophic mind-set.

My base had a really limited phone and internet service. We were allowed one call and thirty minutes of internet time a week. Due to the time difference, every time I tried to call my mum, I was told she wasn't feeling great and she would be resting. The negative thought system really kicked in then. The last time I saw my mother was twelve months before this. We lived five-hundred miles apart and only had phone contact for the previous six months due to my work and life commitments.

I remember her as happy and healthy, having a normal weight for a woman her size. Nothing could prepare me for the sight which met me when I arrived at her door. It felt very early and quiet. The street and the house had never been so silent. In my mind, I felt like I was walking into an ambush. That was my gut feeling letting me know something was amiss. It wasn't wrong.

My beautiful wee mammy was sitting wrapped up on the sofa, with a blanket over her legs and her tiny, frail feet sticking out at the bottom. Her wee West Highland white terrier curled up by her side. The second I walked into the room, my breath left my body. I couldn't think. I couldn't focus. I couldn't believe what my wee mammy looked like. She was lucky if she was 80 lbs. Her face was drawn. She was pale and weak, and her night clothes didn't fit anymore. It was a moment which will haunt me for the rest of my life.

That moment I had my first ever anxiety attack.

My wee mammy had cancer. It had ravaged her body. She looked like a different person from the one I had last seen. I fell to my knees and begged God not to let this be true. Please God, I am begging you; don't let this be my wee mammy. I knew in a heartbeat that she would be taken from me. I started crying hysterically and my wee mammy forced herself to sit up.

She said, "Come here, son. It's OK, I am OK. Don't be silly, I am OK, I promise."

I curled up and put my head on her knee. I could feel her kneecap pressing on my temple. She put her hand on my head and said, "Don't be upset, son. It's OK, I am going to be OK. I have you back now; everything's going to be OK."

The fire from her once-sharp temper and voice was gone. It was peaceful. I couldn't tell you how long I sat with my head on her knee but it felt like it a lifetime. My wee mammy knew she was going to die. She knew and I knew, and the only thing I could do was cry. I couldn't get off my knees. I couldn't breathe. She asked if I wanted my sister to come over and sit for a while. Maybe she could explain everything, and let me go outside for a wee bit to see if I could calm down. I agreed and my sister arrived.

A look says everything. My sister knew the same as I did. This was a fight my mum wasn't going to win.

One of the most memorable things that day was feeling physically and mentally drained. I felt as if I had gone ten rounds with a heavyweight boxer. Every muscle hurt. Even my eyes were sore. Panic and anxiety attacks can be so powerful that they leave you washed out. But I had no choice. I had to face reality. The woman who cared for me, loved me unconditionally, and made me the person I am today was six weeks away from death. She was being taken from me and I wasn't ready. But the stages of grief were not to be played out yet. I remember thinking, *if this lady has six weeks to go, then I need to be focused. I need to be strong. I can't have her last memory of me as a nervous wreck. I can't show anxiety, panic and fear.*

I said I needed to go. I just kept saying it. I ran out of the front door and threw up. My eyes lost focus. It felt like someone had stolen the breath from my body. I couldn't regain control. I remember feeling panicky and agitated. It felt like a brass band was marching up and down inside my chest. I struggled to breathe. I panicked. My mum's neighbour thought I was having a heart attack. I held onto my chest and tried to breathe. This was a full-on anxiety attack and it wasn't going to be my last one. I would suffer these attacks for many years. In the short gaps between my rapid breathing, I kept asking:

Why is this happening? Please God, take me instead. Please take me! I am not afraid of death; in fact, I welcome it. This is not fair! But it wasn't my time and He didn't answer me that day. I couldn't even stay in the same street right then. My partner picked me up in the next street and drove me to the place I was staying. I thought I was about to die. The more I thought about it, the worse the feelings became. They wouldn't go away. That only lasted between six and seven minutes. It felt like a lifetime.

She was my wee mammy. I was about to fight anxiety on a level I didn't even know existed at this point. But I was also fighting hers for her. We had lost my brother a few years before and my mother died inside that day. No question. She never recovered, and the fire and sparkle she possessed faded and was replaced with sadness and dullness behind her eyes. She never shone brightly again.

One of the most amazing things I saw was the acceptance she had. She didn't try to fight it. She didn't say, "No, this is not over." She held my hand tight and whispered, "It's OK, Kevin, my time here is finished; it's time to go and see your brother now." I realised then that it was that easy for her. The comfort she took in her faith was so powerful and amazing that I have yet to see it repeated.

However, this was the calm before the storm.

First, I had to deal with the daily anxiety attacks. I never switched off. I didn't sleep properly for the next six weeks. This was something I was going to get used to. But I didn't want my mother upset by my sadness and constant anxiety, so I remained in a mode that served me well. I remained calm in front of everyone. I was focussed and very protective of my mother. I made sure no one cried in front of her or got too sad. She felt only pure, unconditional love for her remaining time.

When she slept or after everyone had gone, I let everything wash over me. The physical and mental symptoms of anxiety took hold. I think I held out quite well. For most of the time, I would try and hold my breath. I would ground myself and hope that the feelings would go. At other times, I would pretend I heard the front doorbell and escape to the hallway. There, I let the attack come. Then I would recover and go again. It continued like this for the next six weeks. Having anxiety as a crippling emotion didn't worry me because all my thoughts lay with my mum or at least that's what I told myself at the time.

She was always on medication. One of those medications was an anti-anxiety tablet she had taken for years. She was OK while she was still capable of swallowing a tablet, so the doctors kept her on these. They also increased a beta blocker to try and enhance her last stages. She refused all other options. The most painful part was when my mum wasn't capable of oral medication and had to have automated injections. Two medications which couldn't be given any more were the beta blockers and the anxiety medication. These stopped and the change was instant. It was like someone had flipped a switch on the anxiety overdrive.

My mum's anxiety and behaviour changed overnight. She couldn't settle. She lost focus. The agitation was something I have never seen before. The medical practitioners said it was part of the final process. She was on a care pathway and this was normal. Let me assure you this level of anxiety was not normal in any way, shape or form. No one could help. I remember thinking, *I wish I could just add her anxiety on top of mine.* I would gladly have taken the discomfort, panic and agitation for her.

Watching someone suffering with that level of anxiety and being unable to help was heart-breaking. Now, if I am helping anyone with anxiety, before I meet my client, I close my eyes and remember my mother. I begin helping with her memory foremost in my mind. This levels me and reminds me why I am so passionate and focused about anxiety treatment and therapy.

As strange as it may sound, the fact that my mother was given six weeks to live wasn't a big deal. It didn't affect her in any way. At first. But when anxiety came calling it ripped her last few weeks on this planet to pieces. She was either too hot or too cold. Lack of noise would send her agitation into overdrive. Too much noise would do the same. Everything made her agitated and anxious. No-one could help, or even tried. Crippling anxiety tore her apart every hour of the day.

I will never forget the impact anxiety had on the last few weeks of my mother's life. I haven't said this before. During the first stages, I hoped, wished and prayed for more time. I prayed for it not to be true. But towards the end, when anxiety became so painful for her, I hoped, wished and prayed that enough was enough. She had fought her own fight in her own way. I prayed and hoped for the opposite. I wished that she would close her eyes and find peace. I wanted her to be with my brother.

After a few more days like this, my mother passed away in her sleep. I had nothing to be strong for. I was numb and empty apart from one simple emotion. Anxiety. It would remain in my life for many years to come, with one twist after another.

It doesn't matter how hard you try to outrun anxiety, ignore it, or focus on other things. Unless you deal with it, it won't go away. You can mask it and dull it with medication from your GP, but that won't fix it. It's like covering a clock to stop it telling the time. When you lift the cover the clock is still there, ticking away. It's the same for anxiety.

If I had learnt what it was and dealt with it, I could have become anxiety-free many years before I did. But having had it on such a severe level, I know how to help you defeat it. You will re-train your mind. You will adjust your behaviour to ensure that when it's gone, it's gone. And it won't come back

3

So What Exactly Is
Anxiety, and Why Me?

Here is the first thing to remember. When you arrived on this earth, you were born with two fears installed. Loud noises and the fear of falling. Yes, that's right. Look at babies. They will crawl downstairs, stick their fingers in plug sockets, and put all sorts of objects in their mouths: they really are fearless[3].

And that's how we all started out. Everything else has been taught, shown or externally learned.

One of the most debilitating is, of course, anxiety. But you were taught and shown that at some point. How would it be if you could reset your existence? What if you could return to the point where you didn't worry about anxiety, panic or fear? Life would be pretty good, right? So what is anxiety and why has it came calling for you? First, we will look at the different types of anxiety and the emotional repercussions. Feeling anxious about events and situations is normal. This shouldn't be confused with the overwhelming feeling of anxiety that controls your every waking moment. If you feel anxious most of the day for no particular reason, or have irrational fears which result in you being unable to live a normal life, then you could have an anxiety disorder.

There are various anxiety disorders. Here is a look at the most common one and the symptoms that go along with it.

(GAD) General Anxiety Disorder: General anxiety disorder is defined as being when you suffer excessive worry and fear for more than four to six months, along with a minimum of three of these symptoms[4].

1. Problems falling asleep/shutting off.
2. Irritability.
3. Tension.
4. Tiredness/fatigue.
5. Lack of focus/concentrating.
6. Over concerned/worry about all things.

Other signs can include physical symptoms such as:
- Excessive sweating.
- Feeling faint. Headaches. Shaking. Tightness of chest.
- Heavy feeling in the pit of stomach. Panic attacks.
- Nausea.
- Loss of appetite.
- Hyperventilation.

Along with Psychological symptoms such as:
- Impatience.
- Easily distracted.
- Sense of dread, worry and panic. Over sensitive.
- Thinking you can never get better. Fear of illness.
- Fear of accidents.
- Feelings of isolation and bewilderment. Wanting to escape from situations.
- Paranoia. Thinking everyone can see you have anxiety.

These symptoms and issues can easily lead to a panic attack and they come with no warning. They happen as a rapid build-up of overwhelming emotions and fears and can include several of the following:

- Fast/pounding heartbeat. Dizziness.
- Feeling faint. Nausea. Sweating.
- Shortness of breath. Chest pains.
- Involuntary shaking and twitching. Overwhelming feeling of danger or fear.

Social Anxiety Disorder: It's pretty normal to feel nervous and have a touch of anxiety in new social circles, interacting with people you haven't met before or know anything about. Public speaking at meetings or work places, wedding speeches and formal occasions can cause varying levels of anxiety. For people with Social Anxiety Disorder – some even call it social phobia – this often leads to severe and very intense anxiety and panic. The fear of being judged, criticised or made fun of often heightens the level. Everyday situations like eating in front of people can be affected. The signs and symptoms are very similar to GAD. For social anxiety, often the physical symptoms are more intense and overpowering when someone thinks about the upcoming event they will be attending. But physiological symptoms are just as debilitating. Added to the lists above for social anxiety is:

- Blushing.
- Stammering/speech impediments. Nausea.
- Diarrhoea.
- Excessive perspiration.

If you suffer from social anxiety you will try to avoid all social situations where you think these will happen. You worry that everyone can see you and your anxiety, when no one can see any worry, stress or strain going on inside the body and mind. If you can't avoid the occasion, you will attend but feel extremely agitated throughout. You won't enjoy it. Your whole focus will be the anxiety. At the earliest opportunity, you will leave. This can have serious side-effects for sufferers and the people around them, especially if they are young and need parents, friends or family to support them. Personal relationships will crumble quickly. It can affect your skills as a parent and work colleague. People often give up employment to be alone and focus on dealing with their social anxiety.

Panic Disorder: Panic disorder is an anxiety disorder characterised by reoccurring unexpected panic attacks. Panic attacks are sudden periods of intense fear. They may include palpitations, sweating, shaking, shortness of breath, numbness, or a feeling that something really bad is going to happen. This is different from social anxiety disorder.

Agoraphobia: Fear of being somewhere which would be difficult or embarrassing to get out of if you had a panic attack.

Avoiding places or situations where you fear you might have a panic attack, or experiencing great distress in such places.

Post-Traumatic Stress Disorder (PTSD): A condition which can occur after a person has experienced a traumatic event involving intense fear and threat of bodily injury or death. Examples include military combat, sexual assault or natural disasters.

Obsessive Compulsive Disorder (OCD): Unwanted and disturbing thoughts, images, or urges (obsessions) which intrude into a child/teen's mind. These cause a great deal of anxiety or discomfort, which the child/teen then tries to reduce by engaging in repetitive behaviours or mental acts (compulsions).

Any of these can be set off for a number of reasons. Every behaviour you use has a positive intention behind it. That might seem a strange statement to make, but read on and I will explain exactly what I mean. Notice I said a positive intent and not a positive behaviour. Everyone is different, but the majority of panic attacks can last anywhere between two and five minutes. I will teach you how to block and defend against them at the early onset stage.

So what is going on: The biggest player in all of this is the most powerful element in your whole mind – the subconscious. The subconscious is an amazing, powerful tool. You take it for granted on a daily basis and overlook its importance. It takes care of the majority of your thoughts, feelings and behaviours. In fact, it is responsible for up to ninety percent of your thinking and behaviour.

The subconscious mind belongs to you and you alone. Everything it does, happens with a very strong positive intention behind it. It will never hurt, damage or knowingly cause pain to you. Everything it does has a strong positive intention behind it. That includes the anxiety, worry and fear you are feeling. The behaviour part, however, is where the worry, fear and anxiety come from.

Conscious mind 10%

- Will power
- Long-term memory
- Logical thinking
- Critical thinking

Subconscious mind 90%

- Beliefs
- Emotions
- Habits
- Values
- Protective reactions
- Long-term memory
- Imagination
- Intuition

So the intention is good, but the behaviour it has picked up on to enforce the positive intent is wrong. For example, if you lack confidence because of certain beliefs you have about yourself (which are stored in your subconscious mind) then you might start to feel anxious around people. That anxiety will stop you putting yourself in new situations and around new people. If you don't do that, then you stay safe and protected. You can't be hurt by negativity, for example. The intent has a strong positive intention behind it – to keep you safe and protected – but the behaviour it has adopted is the wrong behaviour for you. Instead of spending hours in talking therapy (not to mention the cost involved), why don't you just go straight to the subconscious mind and change the behaviour? You can decide that part for yourself. I will go straight to the behaviour change at the subconscious level every time. Let me explain why.

So many people come to me with the same story: they have been in talking therapy for a while and haven't made any real progress. (Although talking based therapy, and other forms of therapy, do have their place. Every person is different and needs a different approach).

Instead of talking everything over, re-living the negativity and experiencing the pain and turmoil which caused the problem, I go straight to the subconscious and change the process and behaviour. I use NLP techniques that are tried, tested and proven to be highly effective in the majority of cases. It is like opening a brand new cell phone all clean and in perfect working order with minimum apps and no confusion. I take away all the negative apps and go back to factory settings where everything is simplified and easier to use and understand. In this case, I remove the limiting beliefs and behaviours causing the problems. You keep the positive intention, and you change the behaviour. As for the 'why me?' part of the question, well, anxiety can be forged over years of experiences. In fact, any experience you've ever had can cause an anxiety disorder.

Most anxiety disorders develop in childhood and young adulthood, through experience and learned behaviour. But, like any emotion or experience, it can be a learning tool and not a crippling, damaging one. No-one has defined exactly why anxiety happens. It is an emotion given by the subconscious element of your mind, and the intent behind it is always a positive one. It's just the behaviour part it has gotten wrong.

Anxiety is not something you are born with. It is something you learned or were shown and taught. So now I want to teach you something new: two methods of beating anxiety and panic attacks before they take hold. These are called blockers. They are designed to stop you escalating your emotional state leading to the panic and anxiety that controls you in that moment. They allow you to take steps to stop things escalating in your own mind as it were.

The first one is called calm anchoring.

The purpose of calm anchoring is to allow you to go back to a calm and clear state, before limiting thoughts or feelings take hold of you. It's the reverse of an emotional trigger. For example, have you noticed that if you have a bad memory of an incident, person, or ex-partner, that a smell, certain location, sound or song instantly takes you back to it? It is just like that, but you are going to reverse the effect. You will choose a calm, good, strong feeling to focus on. You get to be the trigger; although I call it an anchor. Again, this takes time, patience and practise, and the more you do it the stronger and more instant it becomes.

I recommend that you use this when that first little flutter comes your way. Panic and anxiety attacks are predominantly three-fold:

- The inkling (that flutter of something out of balance).
- The take hold (full symptoms kick in with force).
- The dissipation (your breathing and body start to slow down; leaving you shaken)

Many people have asked what to do on the second stage. The strongest advice I have is to attack it at the first stage with vengeance and vigour. With panic and anxiety attacks, action is so much better than reaction.

The first stage is where you change the behaviour and control the next few minutes of your life. You will know what I mean by the first flutter. Your breathing flows out of sync. The heavy, churning, dark feeling in your stomach or chest starts to show itself. You know it's about to come on full-force. You see what's coming and you can hear the panic in your inner voice telling you, "Oh, crap, here it comes." Everything slows, but you are stuck in the same place.

That's exactly where you hit back and change the outcome. So here goes, you feel the first step arrive and you know what is about to happen, like a car a mile away coming closer and closer until it hits you. What you do is side-step and let that car drive right by, without one ounce of emotion involved. With one press, you activate your calm anchoring button. For this example you are going to use a sharp press on the index finger and thumb to set the anchor. That motion will then return when it is repeated, whenever you need it. Let's show you how to calm anchor.

First, using either hand, place your index finger and thumb together, with no real pressure.

When you feel ready, close your eyes and follow the following steps:

34

1. Get comfortable and gently close your eyes.
2. Start with a few deep breaths and, as you exhale, drop every muscle in your body. Repeat a few times until you feel calm and relaxed.
3. You can recall any experience you like. You have complete control over your memories.
4. I want you to think of a memory when you were at your calmest. This can be a holiday, event, or being in a relationship. Somewhere you can remember feeling peaceful and calm.
5. Now really think and focus on that experience. See what you saw during that time. Feel the way you felt. Hear what you heard during that event. Really re-live as if it were happening right now. Enjoy it. Go all the way into it until you feel the same way now as you did then.
6. Once you are really in that moment, take a breath inwards for three seconds. On the pause, just before you exhale, press inwards three to five times with your thumb and index finger. This will anchor that state.
7. Slowly exhale and repeat the anchoring process.
8. When you feel that state has been anchored, gently open your eyes and relax those fingers.
9. You have now created a strong, calm anchor. This will take you back to that state when you press on it.
10. Whenever you feel that flutter come anywhere near you, simply close your eyes, take a breath, and press that anchor. You are transported to the amazing, calm, relaxed state. Sit with it for a moment and enjoy it. You have now defeated your first anxiety/panic attack. That is something worth smiling about.
11. When you have enjoyed your moment, smile and carry on with whatever you were doing.

The second method is called STOP NOT TODAY. This method uses a therapy called TFT by the brilliant Roger J Callahan[5].

This method uses one of the key meridian points on the body. The inside of the hand. It is the first point in the nine point TFT process, or, as it is more commonly known, tapping. I will look at the full method and benefits of tapping later in the book. For now, you will use a very small part to push away any anxiety or panic attacks. This is an effective and beneficial exercise. Your body is filled with energy, life, and a deep understanding of the self-healing processes. Tapping allows you to access that powerful ability to heal.

Again, the key thing to remember is that it's all about stage one. At this stage we can make the most effective impact on what's coming and cut stage two dead before it takes hold.

The first thing you do when you feel the stage one flutter coming is:

1. Close your eyes.
2. In your loudest inner voice shout STOP.
3. Take the karate chop part of your inner hand and turn it towards yourself.

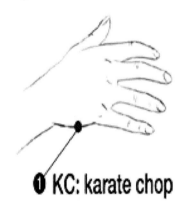

❶ KC: karate chop

4. Take two fingers on the opposite hand and tap on that point.
5. The Tapping is done with two or more fingertips. This covers a larger area and makes sure you reach the correct point.
6. While you can tap with the fingertips of either hand, most people use their dominant hand. Right-handed people tap with the fingertips of their right hand while left-handed people tap with the fingertips of their left hand.

7. A simple phrase will work best with this one: "Not today panic and anxiety. I am far too strong for you, now go away."

8. After repeating this phrase as you tap, for around sixty to ninety seconds, stop. Take a look around your internal self. Stage one will have dissipated.

We are all different and perhaps one of these methods of stopping panic and anxiety attacks will work better for you than the other. Try out both to find your own personal preference. Repetition is key as always. You are re-writing old behaviours and thought patterns, and this won't be done if you only do this once. Don't be half-hearted. Give this everything you have, every time you try it and keep practicing it. You get to pick your new behaviour patterns and habitual behaviour, but conquer this exercise and you really set it in stone.

I used both methods in my battle and I love both methods equally. I need you to have a level of self-belief and desire that it is unparalleled to anything you've had before. The battle to defeat anxiety will be decided by the amount of time and effort you put into the fight. Anxiety always throws everything it has at you. Instead of hoping, wishing and praying for it to change and go away, why don't you do things differently and throw everything you have, and then some, straight back at it?

I know in my heart of hearts that each person, no matter what position they are in right now, can take their inner strength, the desire to beat this, and completely destroy it on every single level. Anxiety is relentless. It doesn't give you warning. It comes when it feels like it, so why don't you do the same? Now I will give you the answer to the same question.

Q: What is anxiety and why me?

A: Anxiety is an emotion which you will own completely, in every way, shape and form. And as for 'Why me?' – simply because you are strong enough to beat it.

4

How Do You Tackle Anxiety?

The first thing I will do is answer the question.

You use your self-healing, your drive, your motivation, your desire to heal and to get better, and you put them all together. You attack it head-on with everything you have. You don't stop until you are in a place where anxiety doesn't rule the day. We all have self-preservation stored inside us. Even if you feel you no longer have yours, it is simply lost for the moment and not forever. The first thing is to remember that you have your future in your hands. No one else controls it.

Read that answer a few times.

Now answer this: How many times have you picked the destination before you have finished the journey?

At times you are your own worst enemy, especially around your own thoughts and the future. Most of the time, your final destination doesn't meet the expectations of the reality. It knocks you down, makes you overthink and over-analyse everything. My advice is plain and simple, stop overthinking. Life is what it is. Sitting for days, weeks and months, mulling over the outcome of something which has already passed isn't going to change it. Also, it won't improve your current situation.

You need to be realistic and not over-dramatize everything. You need to see things for what they are and not what you want them to be. You need to look at what you have instead of what you don't. You need to think about everything with more positivity. So how do you do this? How do you change thoughts and ideas of the ideal future, when they consume you and cause you to feel disappointed when they don't turn out as they should?

The answer is simple. Positive mental attitude and knowledge.

How many people know what anxiety is and why it's happening? This is one of the fundamental reasons why you go straight to flight mode when 'fight or flight' is triggered. Imagine walking into a room and before you stands a wild animal. Its eyes are locked on you, ready to attack. You panic, freeze, start to shake and then try your best to get the hell out of there as fast as you can. You do not know its capabilities, its strengths and its weaknesses, how to tackle it, or even how to beat it. So, you go straight to flight mode.

It's the same for anxiety. Most of the time we don't understand it. Why it is happening, how to tackle it, defeat it, what its weakness is and how we triumph. It is no different from the physical example of the wild animal. We are all afraid of things.

We don't know and have no idea how to beat. When anxiety comes, that is the main reason why you almost instantly go into flight mode. Remember you are doing things differently now. You are becoming educated in the field of anxiety. You are learning how to fight back and how to get smart. You are going to make the switch from flight to fight mode.

One of the key parts to this is relating anxiety to something you know.

Relate to a blister: This may sound strange, but it allows you to see anxiety in a different light. When you have a blister on the back of your foot, it is a really good thing. If the blister didn't happen, the shoe would rub past the skin into the flesh, and then directly on the bone, and that would cause irreversible damage to the foot. But before you get to that stage the body has developed a blister, sending a signal to the brain and letting you know something is not right and needs fixing.

Without that sharp pain and uncomfortable blister, how would you know something was wrong before it was too late? Anxiety serves the very same purpose. It's your internal system of thoughts, feelings and emotions, telling you that something is not right on the inside. Something is off-key or out of balance and you need to fix it. You need to deal with the problem, because if you don't, that anxiety is simply not going anywhere. So, yes, anxiety is nothing more than an internal blister and you know how to fix it. You go from the inside out. You fix, heal and mend like never before.

Realise that you get to control your reactions: You create your outside reality by the thoughts and beliefs you maintain about life in general. What you believe in your inner world, you see in your outer world – not the other way around. We all have problems, and we're often tested by circumstances outside of our control. Even though you may not be in control of what's going on outside you, you most definitely can control your reaction to those situations. You have the power. Your inner world (cause) affects the influence you allow the outer world (effect) to have on you. So, next time you hear somebody mention that you have great personal power, know they are one hundred percent correct. You have more control than you think.

Love who you are: No one is better qualified to set you on the right path, or point you in the right direction, as you. You know yourself better than anyone else in the entire world. You are unique. You are different. You are special. Embrace that part and love with a passion. Enjoy who you have become. You may not be everyone's cup of tea, but you are someone, and you should have so much self-love that this builds, and gives you the confidence and the courage of your convictions to do the right thing for you.

Take responsibility: At any moment, your attitude can be that of a victim or the creator. The first step you need to shift from victim to creator is to take responsibility.
Here's the attitude of a creator:

- I create my life.
- I am responsible for me.
- I'm in charge of my destiny.

When you teach yourself this, everything appears with more clarity. This allows you to adjust your next move accordingly. People can suggest, inform and even try and push you into making choices, but only you can actually make them. You are your own person. Take some responsibility. Stand-up. Be strong.

Do what your heart and gut are telling you to do, and don't try and shift the blame when anything goes wrong.

Steamroll the bullies in life: I am not talking about violence or physical harm. I am talking about the one tool you have that a negative person doesn't. A great outlook, and strong minded opinion and approach. Nothing scares a negative person more than meeting someone who has it in place. Someone who has a plan and a solution. Someone who has everything ready to move forward. They won't even suggest negativity towards you if they see how strong, confident and self-assured you are. Push straight through them with no thought as to how they perceive you. Life is not a dress rehearsal. This is the real deal. Stop letting negativity affect you and embrace the moment. Live it as if every day were your last. I promise you won't regret it.

Stop expecting life to be easy: Life gets tough at times. For all of us. It can even be painful. But you're brave, resourceful and you can take it. Know that sometimes things won't be easy, and adopt the attitude that you have what it takes to deal with anything life throws at you. If you become like the modern generation and expect everything handed to you gift-wrapped, then you're in for a disappointment. Have realistic expectations. Of course, set the standards bar high, but also have realistic expectations, especially of other people. Not everyone can manage these things we've talked about. There will always be people to remind you about disappointment and failure. I refer you back to the paragraph above.

I once read: 'Our attitude towards life determines life's attitude toward us', and that is very true. Stop thinking every twist and turn is a negative. Some of the most important lessons in life have transpired through negative actions. The trick is to learn from them and move on. You honestly do become what you think. I promise you one million percent, that if you take life on its own terms and learn and grow from it, life can be one hell of an experience, folks.

The biggest factor with anxiety is lack of happiness. Allowing other people to make you happy in life. Once you master the art of becoming and maintaining happiness, things look very different. Happiness is not theirs to have, to look after and to control. Because it is not theirs, inevitably they will mess it up, and, in most cases, break it. Your happiness belongs to you and should be determined by you and you alone. Giving that much power to someone is always going to end in failure. Let me explain why.

Happiness is one of our most valued emotions: Happiness is something we experience and grow to love and enjoy. It is much better than the other emotions which wash over us day to day. In a balanced life, it is the one that is most prominent. It is the one which keeps us smiling and looking forward to life. It should be cherished and nurtured and cared for every day. It is your job and yours alone to make sure that happens.

Others add, they don't make: I have heard many people say they just want someone to make them happy. Here is a news flash – you are looking in the wrong place. The only person your happiness should be dependent upon is yourself. If you are looking for someone else to make that happen, it really isn't. Other people may come along in life and add to your happiness, but to count on them and depend on them to make it happen, is destined to fail from the get-go. You control your own happiness and you are as happy as you decide to be, regardless of the circumstances surrounding you. You choose to be unhappy, you choose to be down and you blame the circumstances or others for it. The fact remains that you cannot control another person's flawed actions, but you definitely can control your reaction and you are defined by your actions. So remember, you are in charge of your happiness and you allow others to add to it, but definitely not define it.

Happiness by change, not chance: We have all heard the saying, 'If at first you don't succeed, try, try again.' Well, that isn't true in any way, shape or form. How about you do this instead?

If at first you don't succeed, change the behaviour or method and then try again.

Determination and perseverance will only take you so far. If what you are doing and the way you are doing it isn't working now, or in the past, then it's not going to work in the future. If you are unhappy, then you need to look at what you are doing and identify the behaviour or the action causing it. Then you change that and go again. Honestly, you will be so surprised at the outcomes if you change tack and go at it in a different way. Remember, happiness by change, not chance. The key word here is change.

You are as happy as you want to be: This is something my mother used to tell me every time I was sad or down and at the time I didn't see it. I didn't understand it or even listen, but it is definitely valid. We are emotionally-lead beings and, as I got older and slightly wiser (some would say not so much), I learned that this statement is very true. In fact, it's spot on. Let me explain why. Words will always equal a thought, and a thought will always equal an emotion, so how you use your self-talk is vital. Try this out for size:

Close your eyes and tell yourself something good about yourself or something good you have achieved in life. (And, yes, everyone has something; even a divorce petition if that's where your mind takes you) Did you catch it? Yes, that was called a smile. No matter how big or small, really concentrate on the feeling that the positive statement gives you. Go on, do it again, and really concentrate and, yes, this time you can catch yourself smile.

Now tell yourself something bad about yourself. Notice that heavy feeling in the pit of your stomach, your chest, neck, or wherever it hits you. Notice the two distinct feelings. All because of the words you choose to speak. The message here is a really simple one. Talk to your inner self the same way as you would to your children or a loved one. You wouldn't put them down, tell them they can't or belittle them all day long, so my question is; why are you doing it to yourself?

Change the negative for powerful and positive. A good example is as follows:

I DON'T KNOW WHAT IS GOING TO COME AT ME TODAY, BUT I ASSURE YOU I WILL FACE IT HEAD-ON, AND GIVE IT EVERYTHING I HAVE.

So, just for today, let's do it differently and just be bloody kind to yourself for once.

Happiness is such a beautiful, all-consuming emotion. You are doing yourself an injustice in life by not having it. So please remember, today you will be as happy as you choose to be, and it WILL come by change not chance.

5

Anxiety: The Best Form of Defense Is Attack

The title really does say everything. Think back to fight or flight mode now to beat and change your relationship with anxiety. You already know that you need to behave differently and to think differently. You need to continue this battle, and the best form of defence is attack. You are not going to sit by and allow these feelings to control what you do, how you think, and how you behave.

One of the major tools you have is an extremely effective NLP technique which is used worldwide. I call it parts integration. I have shown you two blocking methods already. Now I will take it a step further and show you how to integrate. But first, I want to expand on the brief description I gave about your subconscious. The more you understand how and why it does what it does, the easier it is to use all the methods and techniques I show you in the book. If these are used correctly and given everything you have, then your anxiety is definitely on its last legs.

Most people aren't aware of the subconscious mind, its power, or exactly how it works, but it is the main engine room in your mind. It is the part which contains and stores all the information you are currently unaware of, so here are a few things you need to know about the subconscious in all its powerful glory:

The subconscious mind is primal. It focusses on emotion instead of reason. It's where your primal instincts stem from.

Studies suggest that the subconscious mind processes about four hundred billion pieces of information per second, and the impulses travel at a speed of up to 100,000 mph. Now compare this to your conscious mind, which processes only about two thousand pieces of information per second, and its impulses travel only at 100-150 mph.

The subconscious mind sees no difference between what's real and what's imagined. If it has it, then it takes it for real.

Whatever you feed it, the subconscious mind believes to be fact. It can't differentiate between truth and a lie; past or present. Everything it deals with, it takes as present time and understands to be true.

The subconscious mind can be altered. It can be re-programmed with new habits, beliefs and behaviours and allowed to use them. However, that is not what the majority of people do with it. Instead, they choose to believe and act out old patterns and emotions.

Visualisation is the best method to re-program your subconscious: Did you know that your subconscious communicates through images and metaphors? That's why dreams are important. Try visualising being anxiety-free instead of just speaking about it. Visualisation works much better.

Your subconscious mind opens more when you are not fully alert: For you to hear or access your subconscious you need to be relaxed. Archimedes' 'eureka' moment was when he was having a bath and in a very relaxed state.

The subconscious mind records everything, awake or asleep. It is like a record button that never switches off.

The subconscious is yours. It will never knowingly do anything which will cause damage or hurt. Think about it like this: if you woke standing on the edge of a cliff, what is the first thing you would do? Well, instantly step back, I would think. So, would you think about stepping back, or would it just happen? That is your subconscious. When you hear a noise in the middle of the night and you wake startled, again this is your subconscious. Even when you make a cup of coffee, your subconscious does it all and it does it at lighting speed without you even having to think about it.

Now, hopefully, you can see just how very powerful the subconscious is. That's where your thoughts, beliefs, patterns, habits and emotions sit. When it comes to anxiety, they are automated now by the subconscious.

The subconscious can be re-programmed by two methods. One I have already spoken about and will go into more detail later in the book. The majority of therapies dealing with anxiety use this one method of visualisation and repetition. They question your limiting thoughts and beliefs and use the conscious mind to adapt and embrace new patterns and habits. The second way is much more direct. This method isn't used so widely as the first. But if it is performed correctly, it is just as powerful – if not more so – than the first method. It is called the parts integration.

Parts integration is a well-known NLP method and technique used by practitioners and hypnotherapists around the world. It does exactly that: integrates the issue. With anxiety, the intent behind the emotion and behaviour – just like with everything the subconscious mind does – is very good. The behaviour and the emotion in question is wrong, so you go to the subconscious and you change that part. You look at it, feel it and act differently towards it. This allows us to change and replace the anxiety with a much more positive, healthy behaviour.

I know only a handful of people who are capable of doing this to an extremely high standard, I have been taught by those people, watched them and mastered my own methods on them. Now I am going to teach it to you in its purest form.

I will simply call this the anxiety parts. It is where you go directly to your own subconscious mind, look at the parts causing you damage (i.e. anxiety) and replace it with a new part. A part which doesn't cause damage. Now I want you to do what I call content free. The subconscious mind knows only too well, due to your thoughts and belief system, exactly what you are talking about. You are thinking about the anxiety by reading this and doing this technique, so you can allow yourself to work content-free. Remember, the subconscious works at a much faster rate than the conscious mind. Before you start and go to your subconscious mind from your conscious mind, you need to get a few things in order. I will call these the preliminary measures, before you go to the task.

One of the biggest factors in connecting with the subconscious is that you must be in a fully submerged peaceful and relaxed state, so you will always start the same way. Don't attempt this method in a busy room or anywhere there are distractions such as TV, animals, or disruptions. You need your full undivided attention and focus right now.

You ensure you won't be disturbed, you turn your phone off (not on vibrate: even that noise can throw you off). You ensure that you are in a peaceful setting and you take a breath and give this part every single bit of focus and attention you can muster. Don't do this straight after coming in from work. Don't do this while trying to multi-task. Don't do this when your emotional state means that you can't focus on anything outside the integration. Find yourself a nice comfortable chair with a back rest, keep the upper body straight, and place your hands on your lap with your palms facing upwards.

Parts integration technique self-model:

You take your breathing all the way down, slowing and easing up on your heart rate and going into what is almost a meditative state. Nice, calm, slow breathing is the key. A good example is to breathe in for the count of three, hold for three and then exhale for three. Practice that for a few minutes and just feel your body ease up and relax.

Once you have the breathing sorted, I want you to relax every muscle in your body. Let every single muscle and fibre drop down to the bone, no stress, no tension, no pressure. Focus on your inner self-awareness and drop it all the way down so you are at peace and relaxed.

Using your own internal dialogue, silently in your own mind, very softly, and gently you will begin:

Thank your subconscious mind for all the positive intentions that it holds for you and for always looking out for you, keeping you safe and protected.

Acknowledge that the intention is good and strong but the behaviour it's using is not the best behaviour for you. That's the behaviour you would like to deal with today.

Raise your forearms and hands about six inches directly up from your lap, so they are balanced shoulder-width apart in front of you.

Now speak to the subconscious directly. Ask it to take the part that is damaging and hurting you and place it out on you left hand. Once it has done that you will feel a sign that it has happened. This will be a flicker of the fingers or a feeling of something in your hand.

Now talk to a different part of the subconscious mind. The smart part, the problem-solving part we all have. Ask it to keep the very same intention, but to search for and find a new healthy behavioural part to replace the old one. When it has the new part, tell it you would like it to take that part and place it on your right hand. Again, you don't even need to know what the new part is; you will, however, be aware that your right hand is holding it with a signal. Again, a flicker of the fingers or a feeling that differs from the left hand.

When both parts are out and in the open, you ask the subconscious to take those two parts and move them together. You will notice that your hands gently start to move inwards towards each other. It feels almost as if two small magnets are on your palms pulling them in.

At this point you continue to breathe and relax. You keep your focus on your breathing. Don't worry about what your hands are doing: that's the subconscious' job right now.

This will take as long as it takes. You will notice very small movements now. These movements will occur at the most comfortable rate for you. As the hands draw closer, the new, healthy part seems to increase in strength and power. It gets stronger and stronger, second by second.

Just before the hands move in and touch, you ask the subconscious: does it have any objections to replacing the old part with the new part? Should it object, it will give you a sign by either a flicker of the fingers on the left hand or a feeling.

As the hands move in and touch, that new part sits completely on top. It dominates and diminishes the old part in every single way.

When your hands are now in contact and have finished moving, you ask the subconscious to take the new part and put it all the way back in. You will feel that happen now.

And as the new part is entered and locked into place, you will notice something different. Something has changed. It doesn't matter if you can or can't explain what has just happened. But something feels very different for you.

Don't expect to get it spot on first time, every time. Read the process, practise it in your head and know the sequence. Then it flows and no effort is required. This is an extremely powerful tool in the battle with anxiety. Once mastered correctly, you should notice differences and shifts in your internal set up. Lighter, clearer and different. You will be happy with 'different' for now.

Parts integration really is a massive tool to use in the battle. That's why I have shown the self-technique method in this book. It does take time to learn and practice so I would suggest you do it in bite-size chunks. Firstly, just spend some time on the breathing part and practice that for a while. Breathing properly is a key factor in bringing your relaxation and calmness levels down. It can also be great fun to master. Then you go on to the muscles and relaxation part. Remember, the subconscious mind reacts more effectively to visualisation, so imagine you are looking down on yourself and you have the control button.

Start at the top, working down the forehead, cheeks, eyes, chin and jaw line. Relax and ease up on each in turn. Let the shoulders drop all the way down and allow that feeling to flow through every part of your body. Imagine a warm comfort blanket being wrapped around you from head to toe, and as it touches you, that part just drifts away.

You should discover the same relaxed state you have when you find yourself day dreaming. You enter this state on a daily basis and aren't even aware of it. Have you ever been so engrossed in a book, TV show or movie that when someone speaks to you, you realise you haven't heard a word they say? Before you know it, they are shouting your name and you are saying, "What? I didn't hear you."

This is a very similar process. You are going from being engrossed in a TV show to being engrossed with yourself. Millions of people around the world practise this with yoga and meditation. This works to calm you and gives more awareness of your inner self. When you are in this state you are in the perfect state to communicate directly with the most powerful part of your mind the subconscious.

Using NLP and parts integration is one of the key tools I use with my clients each day. The results and benefits are plain to see when you look at the history of the client. Someone arrives with limiting and damaging beliefs such as: I will never be anxiety free, this is genetic. I was destined to suffer as my parents did before me. If only I could get rid of the anxiety my life would be so much clearer, better and happier. Those words will sound rather familiar to you right now. But remember what I said at the start of this book; this is a new way of behaving, a new way of thinking and a new set of results. So give this section as much focus and energy as you have. Repetition and preparation is key. A very good saying we had in the military is: Prior Planning and Preparation Prevents Piss Poor Performance – or the 7 Ps.

Another extremely important tool is an NLP technique called Reframe. A reframe is where you give another meaning to a statement by recovering more content, which in turn can change the focus. You take a negative behaviour or thought and turn it into the positive by changing the representation of the problem or issue. In other words, all the meanings you have are dependent on your point of view.

The meaning behind any event in life is dependent on how you frame it. If you can change the frame then you change the meaning and your behaviour and reaction to it. For example, dressing up as the grim reaper in fancy dress is fun and scary at Halloween or New Year but distinctly weird at a funeral. The most well-known reframe is the children's story *The Ugly Duckling*. He was picked on for being different and ugly until he compared himself to what he was; a beautiful swan, not a duckling.

Change the frame, change the meaning, and change the attachment to that part. We have many different types of reframe, and there are books just on NLP reframing alone, but the one we are interested in is called content reframing. One of the presuppositions on NLP is that all behaviour has a positive intent. If you look back to the parts integration, we give thanks for the positive intent.

Even when someone behaves in a manner which causes hurt and pain to others, there is always a positive intent behind their actions. It might be to remain in control, to feel safe or even powerful. Look at some of the actions you have taken in the past. You have taken those actions with a positive intention, and even when you hurt someone unintentionally, the behaviour still had a positive intent. Have you ever said harsh words to someone in anger, knowing that those words might upset or hurt them? The reason you do it is not because you are a bad person, but to retain an element of control and gain the upper hand in the situation. You know hurtful words can throw people off balance.

Let's look at a content reframe in your battle with anxiety.

Whenever you take a situation and give it a specific meaning, you are using a content reframe. You might, for instance, acknowledge that you feel agitated when you are thrust into a new situation and are surrounded with people you don't know. However, whether or not it is true, it has now limited your resourcefulness and possible courses of action and outcomes. To reframe this situation you need to ask yourself:

What is the positive intention here? What could this behaviour really mean? For what purpose is this happening? What would I like it to mean?

The first question acknowledges that every behaviour has a positive intention. The second and third questions help you search for alternate meanings that might also be possible. These new meanings could help in this situation. And the fourth question gives you the freedom to choose the meaning you would like to associate with this particular situation.

The positive intention behind it is to keep you in your comfort zone. While you are there, no one can judge or criticise you if you don't say the right things to the right people. That's exactly what the behaviour could really mean. However, ultimately it's up to you what you would like this behaviour to mean. Whatever perspective you take will influence how you feel about the situation and the choices and decisions you make moving forward.

In another example, you might make a generalisation that:

Making a mistake while giving a speech means that I am a hopeless public speaker. Here you are implying that one mistake seals your fate. You have put a meaning to your mistake by indicating that, because of this mistake, you are going to be forever defined as a "hopeless public speaker". In such instances, it is helpful to ask yourself:

What might be useful about this experience? How else could I interpret the meaning of it? What could I potentially learn from the mistake?

What did I do well? What's positive about this situation?

This questioning process encourages you to consider the positive aspects of your behaviour. It helps encourage you to change the way you view the meaning you have attached to this particular experience.

With reframing, it is all about perspectives and your thinking about the event. Anxiety does have a positive intention. You may find it hard to see the intent, but if you really look closely, it is there. It is all about re-looking and re-educating your way of thinking. If you do that then you change the emotional attachment and the feelings involved with it. The key to reframing is: do not take your thoughts as gospel. We all interpret things differently. We usually let our emotions lead us in our reactions. The key here is to stand back and question the meaning and the reasons behind them. Look at the facts and don't let anxiety jade your interpretation of the world and its events.

Remember, this is your life we are dealing with. Happiness can only be achieved by change and that's exactly what we are doing. We are changing. Big time.

6

Internal Dialogue, the Key to Change

Thoughts are not just random things that pop into your head. Every thought starts out with a word. That important internal dialogue you use to guide you every day. The process is simple and will always be as follows:

Words = thoughts, Thoughts = emotions

And as you know, we are emotionally-led beings. We live and die by our emotional state. This emotional equilibrium guides you and structures what kind of day you are going to have. It does this by the feelings you acknowledge the second you open your eyes in the morning. How many times have you awoken to that heavy, dark feeling right in the pit of your stomach? Now, that is the feeling which then tells you – and structures – what kind of day is ahead.

Words (internal dialogue)

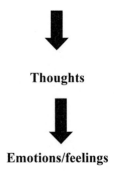

Thoughts

Emotions/feelings

You use these words every day, either with yourself or others. It's how you communicate and let others know how you feel and think. It is one of the most important parts of your internal set-up. All those words come from within. How you use them with yourself is equally important as how you use them with others. More often than not you forget this key element and that's where part of the problem lies. You become focused on people-pleasing or trying to fit in. You forget that the most important person in our life has to be you. If you're not happy, content, at peace, focused, energetic and balanced, how on earth can you make sure loved ones, friends and family are?

You can't make someone feel whatever you're not feeling. You know what you are supposed to be, but that doesn't mean that you are. Let me explain exactly what I mean by this, and show you how your internal dialogue can influence and control your emotional state.

This is called 'times less troubled'.

Phase 1:

The first stage is find somewhere comfortable to sit and give yourself a few moments of peace.

Once you drop down to a nice calm, relaxed state, take the following steps:

- Start off with a deep breath. As you exhale, drop every muscle and fibre in your body. Slow your breathing down to a steady rate.
- Close your eyes, and think of a time when you faced a difficulty in life or focus on a problem or situation with anxiety that didn't sit comfortably with you.
- Remember the feelings you had. Were they feelings of sadness, worry, stress or fear? Did uncertainty lead to anxiety? Or was it a feeling of anxiety from the start?
- See what you observed in that moment. Hear what you heard at the same time and feel that feeling.

Now start to fill in the surrounding details. What time of year was it? What environment were you in? Who was with you? Really focus and re-live that moment.

Scale that feeling from 1-10, and make a note of it. Write down your anxious, painful feeling (1 being low and 10 being high on the scale).

Phase 2:

Take a moment to drain that whole process from your mind. Take as long as you need. Fade it from your thoughts, almost like letting water out of a bath. Let it all drain away as you simply breathe and relax.

Once you are clear, let's go again.

I want you to think of a life which is anxiety-free. It can be anywhere in the world. A vacation, a romantic meal, time with your family or friends. You can use a past location or experience here.

I want you to look down on it and remember that this is the anxiety-free version of you. Notice the smile you are wearing.

See how pain-free you appear. You look relaxed. A healthy glow surrounds you.

Look at the difference in yourself. Look at the amazing level of contentment and happiness you feel. Really focus now and give it your all.

Who is with you? What are you doing? What time of year is it? I want you to listen to all the compliments from people who have seen the old you. "You look amazing." "I knew you would do this." "Well done; you deserve to be back to normal." "You look like a different person."

Really focus on every single aspect and let it sit with you for thirty seconds. Write down your feeling.

Notice it's totally different from the previous feeling. So what changed?

You haven't changed but the words you used to talk to yourself have. That whole internal dialogue is so important. You can sculpt, scope and manage your whole emotional state based on it. You have just managed, in the space of two minutes, to change your entire emotional state and mood. Now you sit and smile as the reality of the words hit home, probably for the first time in a long time.

So, how do you ensure that you change how you use internal dialogue and make it a new pattern and a habitual trait? Well, that's the good part. You have already shown that you can adapt and change your patterns and thoughts based on words. Here's something to keep in mind: when you were born you arrived nearly perfect; I say 'nearly' because you have two pre-installed fears.

Loud noises and falling.

Everything else has been taught or learned, including how you talk to yourself – that important internal dialogue. Do you remember a time when you didn't talk to yourself with negativity and self-doubt? Somewhere along the line you changed that dialogue. Now you are going to change it back.

At a conscious level, I want you to look at the two options. I give you in relation to an imaginary scenario. Again, you are going to use logic and fact over emotional state.

You have been put in charge of a young person between the ages of five and ten. It's your job to take them from where they are now to adulthood. Your biggest tools are your words and the actions associated with those words.

Option 1:

Do you remind them about and focus on, every mistake or failing they come across? Do you predominately use words and statements like:

- You can't do that.
- You're going to fail.
- Don't even bother to attempt it. You're not good enough.
- Save your energy – just accept you will fail.
- You won't ever understand that. Your ideas are stupid.
- Accept your place in life.
- Second place is first loser, and you always fail.
-

OR

Option 2:

You focus on love, compassion, understanding, growth, acceptance, learning, desire, and diligence. You use statements like:

- If you don't try, you won't know.
- Nothing is a failure; everything is a learning opportunity.
- If at first you don't succeed, try a different way and go again. You can do whatever you set your mind to.
- You are always enough. You are perfect as you are.
- We are all created different, that's what makes us unique.
- You can and you will achieve everything you set your mind to.

So what option do you raise and guide this young person with? Well I hope you all pick option 2 and we can look at that in a moment, but for now, let's look at the reality of choosing option 1.

Option 1 is going to do more damage than any stick or stone ever will. You will knock every bit of confidence out of that child from the start. You will cause massive self-doubt, loss of self-esteem and turn what could be a happy-go-lucky young person into a recluse. Someone who chooses to never try and fails before the event or life choice even takes place. You will mentally break the young person and they will have a very hard struggle from that moment onwards.

Option 2, however, gives them self-esteem, boosts confidence, enables understanding of the bigger picture and gives them a drive and determination to attempt everything they want in life. They know that they will always have the fall-back of your love and understanding should things go wrong. It will make them brave and bold enough to attempt anything life throws at them. It is the best way to treat someone with all the love, understanding and compassion in the world.

So my question to you now is:

WHY ARE YOU TREATING YOURSELF LIKE OPTION 1?

And here is the worst part: you believe what we tell yourself. You feel the words you use are true and accurate. You don't usually lie to yourself and if you do, you spot it as a fabrication straight away. Like the therapists of old putting you into a trance and telling you that chocolate tastes bad and you won't eat it anymore. Straight away, the conscious mind spots that as a lie and says, "No, it's not – it tastes good. That's why I keep eating it."

You can never lie to yourself. You believe the inner dialogue you use as true and accurate.

If you are treating yourself like option 1 time after time, you condition yourself to believe it. When you come out with statements like, 'this anxiety is controlling my life' you genuinely believe it. It's what is known as a limiting belief. For any belief to be true, it needs support. The first thing you do is challenge your limiting beliefs and change the internal dialogue you use.

Let's try something a bit different.

Switch over to option 2. Treat yourself and speak to yourself the way you would if you were in charge of a loved one's emotional balance, knowing what you know now. Treat yourself with all the things we have just spoken about. Love, compassion, understanding and passion. If you can't treat yourself like that how are you ever meant to treat anyone else the same way?

How can you experience true, unconditional love and understanding if you don't know what it feels like in the first place? That has to start with you. The rule here is very simple. If you wouldn't treat or speak to a loved one like this then you don't do it to yourself. Everything you do constantly becomes pattern and habit, and right now the pattern and habit for your internal dialogue is on the wrong setting.

Remember – happiness by change and not chance. The anxiety hasn't shifted with what you are doing up until now. So you change behaviour and outcomes and you try again. You will be surprised at how the world looks when you treat yourself with the right kind of love and attention. It all has to start from that internal dialogue. If today has started off on a negative, then do the following positive affirmation. This is where you have a conscious choice of the words you use or the words you start the day with.

I fully understand that you don't love yourself enough to be too full-on with it, but you can change its direction. Have you noticed that when you wake and tell yourself the day ahead is going to be hard-going – the day turns out to be very hard-going? Again, we are pre-determining the outcome before the eventuality. Everything rests on the words you are using. Let me show you how we can adjust, using some very powerful internal dialogue. Take this book with you and find a mirror where you can see the look in your eyes when we do this part. Now I want you to really focus and give this part everything you have. This is a game changer.

Look at yourself in the mirror.

Focus on the look in your eyes, and the expression on your face. Now repeat after me:

I do not know what's coming my way today but I do know that I control it and I will give this day every ounce of energy, focus and fight I have in me.

Now repeat it louder.

And again.

And again.

Now, say it with every bit of passion and drive you can muster. See that look in your eyes changing, that expression getting stronger. You are changing your emotional state with a positive affirmation. Now say it as loud as you can in your head and really give it everything you have. Scream it inside your head if you need to. How strong are you starting to feel? I can feel my whole internal emotional state change as I type this. I am screaming in my head with you. It feels very powerful.

OK, now you're concentrating again and getting you where you need to be.

Do this every morning when you wake, every afternoon and every evening before you retire for the day. You will be surprised by the positive state you can sculpt for yourself. Really go at it every day, until you know every single word comes directly from the soul. Know that you believe it to be true one hundred percent of the time. Using positive affirmations, you are resetting the habitual internal dialogue from option 1 to option 2. It takes repetition and commitment. And then you will have set a new internal dialogue. A positive statement three times a day turns into a belief. The belief turns into a habit. Then the pattern turns into habitual behaviour.

Positive affirmations can be a really powerful tool in re-setting the internal dialogue. The subconscious doesn't work in the past or future. It sees everything in present time so your affirmations have to be linked to the present. If you were to say: "In the future, I will be anxiety-free," it wouldn't be an effective affirmation. Affirmations have to be made in the present context for your subconscious to pick up and believe in them. This allows you to change your internal dialogue. Some really powerful affirmations are:

- I am strong today.
- Today I am in control of my emotions. Today I will not falter.
- I love who I am.
- I will beat whatever comes my way today.

These are all present terms. They are strong statements that you can believe in. They are about the present, not the past or the future. If you think about it, all your internal dialogue is an affirmation. You continually tell yourself what to think and feel, and you believe every word you say. The key is to change the negative self-talk into positive, powerful self-talk and belief. The more you do it, the more you think it, the easier it becomes reality.

With affirmations, have a note pad and pen. Write the affirmation down twenty-five times then stand up, look in the mirror, and say it out loud. You are increasing the use of senses here. You use visual when you read, audio when you talk, and kinaesthetic when you start to feel that you believe what you are saying. You are using every resource available to you and you are doing this two or three times a day. Use it first thing in the morning and last thing at night, so that each day you start and end on a positive.

I recently discovered four notebooks from my battle with anxiety. Looking through them lets me see where I was, how I battled it and where I ended up. I still use positive affirmations first thing every morning and last thing every night. They are extremely powerful when you get into that habitual behaviour and belief about yourself.

You have many limiting beliefs around anxiety in relation to your internal dialogue. A limiting belief is a statement you tell yourself to justify the emotional balance you have. Limiting beliefs can be damaging on an emotional level. You believe these broad statements to be accurate and true. Let me give you an example of a limiting belief and then I will show you how to disprove it.

Muhammad Ali was the greatest boxer who ever lived. That's the belief and it sits as a table top, but for you to support it you need four legs for it to sit on. A table without legs will fall over.

LIMITING BELIEF

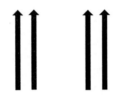

The four legs are statements you tell yourself to support the belief. You need four thoughts or statements to tell yourself in order for that to be true.

A belief isn't a fact. It's a thought you believe in. That doesn't mean it's true. So now you look at your limiting beliefs in turn. Take the belief and support it with four factual reasons or statements (not thoughts, as they can be argued with). You need cold hard facts. For example,

Muhammad Ali lost five professional bouts. On the other hand, Rocky Marciano fought forty-nine professional bouts in his career and won forty-nine. So, based on that fact alone, instantaneously it proves that Ali wasn't the greatest sportsman in the world. Other sportsmen have much better records. Yes, he was a nice person and he was popular – that can't be denied. But the thought that he was the greatest in the history of his sport cannot stand. Factually, it is proven to be one-hundred-percent wrong.

The sun will rise in the morning and set in the evening. That is a fact. It can't be argued with. That is the difference between beliefs and facts. When it comes to your limiting beliefs, you have to go with facts.

Now you look at your own limiting beliefs in relation to anxiety. You pit the belief against the facts. You will have to go a long way to show that your thoughts are a reality.

Let's try one with anxiety:

This anxiety is never going to go away. I am never going to change it. I am stuck this way forever.

That's a common and very strong belief among anxiety sufferers.

<u>ANXIETY WILL NEVER GO AWAY</u>

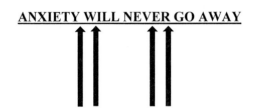

Now look at the legs supporting the belief. Write down four thoughts or reasons which tell you that belief is true.

Let's say one of the thoughts is: 'I have tried everything going to shift it and nothing works.' That's what you tell yourself to support that limiting belief. Now look at that thought factually.

There are over one hundred different ways to tackle anxiety: NLP, hypnotherapy, CBT, EFT, EMDR, havening, alternative medication, health service medication, counselling, private therapy, salt lamps, relaxation, meditation, yoga, reiki, to name only a few. The chances of you trying every single method is extremely slim. So that statement is not true. Everyone is different. We are all unique. Because you tried one way doesn't mean that all other methods will fail.

That statement isn't true anymore.

Take that leg away from the table. Now that limiting belief isn't as strong. It is starting to lose its realism for you.

Now you take the second statement and pit it against fact. Facts are real. They can't be disputed. The objective now is simple:

Take that limiting belief. Take the thoughts and statement you use to support it. Pit them against fact. Fact vs thought. Use every thought. Now see what you have left. If it can't be shown and supported, then it can't be your belief. It has to be looked at again. A different outcome will be taken from the limiting belief.

Everything I have spoken about and tried, started with one thing in common. A word. Words are more powerful than you realise. Even your actions are directed by words, because actions are usually based on the feeling experienced about the task or the activity you are looking at. Happiness by change not chance. This way of thinking is so important. You can change the outcome of everything you do if you get that first part right. The all-important internal dialogue.

You have to look at the facts again. What you have been doing up until now hasn't been working, so you change what you do and try again. It all starts with the vital internal dialogue. It is time to change it.

And finally, it is important to recognise the wrong types of internal dialogue. These can limit and damage us. They are usually broken into four categories. These need to be avoided at all costs; they don't serve any purpose other than to damage and limit us.

Catastrophic: When anxiety raises its ugly head you start to imagine the worst possible outcomes, no matter how absurd they seem. You anticipate the worst possible events, things that would never happen, and you blow them up out of all proportion. These can also trigger anxiety attacks. The important part of this internal dialogue is that anything can turn into a disaster when you least expect it.

Self-critical: This type of internal dialogue involves an ever present and permanent state of self-judgement and negativity over your actions, thoughts and feelings. You can't find any positives and constantly use words like: can't, won't, aren't good enough. You tend to be envious of others who appear anxiety-free around you, and always compare what you are and have to them. This makes you feel as if you are at a disadvantage from everyone around you.

Self-demanding: In this category, you develop exhaustion and stress due to the level of self-expecting perfection. Intolerance to mistakes and failing to know answers increases the negativity around you. This raises your temperament to a shortened state. Internal dialogue will involve words and statements like:

It's not enough. It's not perfect, or it didn't go the way I want and need it to.

This is one of the most negative states to enter with internal dialogue. No matter what you do, you are simply bound to fail, even when perfection is achieved.

Victimising: This type of internal dialogue is summed up with a feeling of hopelessness. This then makes you believe that you can't be fixed. The anxiety will never go away and you are stuck on this crippling cycle forever. It also makes you enter every type of therapy or anxiety treatment with a mind-set of it isn't going to work, before you even give it a try. It isolates you from friends and enforces the victim mentality you have become used to. You won't like the way things are in your life but you won't do anything to change it. You won't give it your all. Words and statements like: no one cares about me, no one values me and why me, will structure your whole mind-set.

The key here is to recognise what your internal dialogue is now. Then do what we spoke about to change that state. When you have practiced and mastered the art of this chapter, you will see the world and anxiety through different eyes. So, go on, get practising. Re-read this chapter as many times as you need to. Make it a new pattern, a new habitual behaviour and the foundation for a whole new you.

7

Negative Thoughts and Beating It

I have talked about and shown you what to do at the first step. That all-important internal dialogue. But what happens if you don't catch it and the thoughts and emotions/feelings take hold and control you before you are even aware of it? Again, you turn to your inner healing. You channel and use your representational system to do that. You see, hear, touch and smell the world around you. These are your fundamental representational systems. They also represent how you think and feel when recollecting an event or action from the past. Have you ever thought back to an event, but felt as if it was happening in the moment because the memory was so real? This is because you can re-live it using pictures, thoughts and sounds. Those are the tools you are going to use. You have five main senses and you are going to tap in to three of them to beat any negative thoughts. The five main senses are:

Auditory System:
You use this for nearly everything you do when communicating, either with yourself or others. Auditory thinking and feeling is a mix of words and other sounds. Sometimes, the anxiety can present as the same message over and over again. This leads you to believe it. That internal dialogue which begins with your words is extremely relevant here.

Visual System:
Here is where you create your visual representation of the past and possible future. You do this by day dreaming, focused visualisation (very popular with competing athletes), fantasising about a different life and what could be and looking to the future. These are all visual system orientated. Have you noticed that

before athletes set off on the race, at the start line they don't even blink? They are using visualisation to go over everything, with the end result being a win. That's why they look so intense in the moments leading up to the start of the event.

Kinaesthetic System:

This is made up of your internal and external touch and bodily awareness. It is where your sense of balance comes from (some studies say this is from what we call the vestibular system). Your emotional balance is the main factor in the kinaesthetic system. For example, when you get a gut feeling about something – that's one hundred percent kinaesthetic. If you can close your eyes and imagine when you were the happiest you have ever been, or imagine and feel placing your hand on a cold sheet of ice, then you would be using the kinaesthetic system. Remember the words = thoughts = feelings? Your kinaesthetic system utilises the feelings part of the process.

Olfactory System:

This is created from smell – both created and remembered. This system won't play much of a part in defeating the negative thoughts, although it might act as a trigger in relation to memories.

Gustatory System:

This one is made up of created and remembered states. A memorable meal would be the case here. Again, like the olfactory, this won't play a major role in the battle. The last two systems were solely for the purpose of explaining the five senses.

The three we are interested in come under the banner: A V K – Audi Visual Kinaesthetic. You use them to beat the negative thoughts which creep past when you are least expecting it. Or when you are focused on your battle with anxiety. The first part you use is accessing the cues you give yourself. The representational system will show itself with cues. For example, eye movement, your body language, the way you hold yourself, the breathing cycle you adopt in the situation. These are all known as access cues and can give a strong indication of your dominant representational system. We all have a dominant representational system but we are not just one system. Most people are a mixture of two and, in some cases, all three.

The trick is to find out which one is kicking in when anxiety comes. Those thoughts will lead to emotions and feelings. You need to know what system is taking hold of you. Then you can use that system to beat it and change the emotion to the thought. Another key is what words you use and you will look at those in detail shortly. For example, if your anxiety takes hold and you keep hearing the same message of 'you will fail', you wouldn't try to beat that audio system with a visual exercise. It simply wouldn't work. You need to access the system and use it against itself.

Now we will look at the main access cues for the way your body responds and thinks.

Eye accessing cues (visual):

These are also known as lateral eye movements or LEM. These are the most distinct and common eye movements you exhibit.

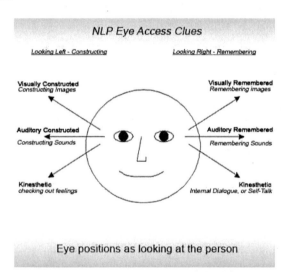

Eye positions as looking at the person

Remembered images and sounds will usually be to the person's right-hand side, with feelings down to the left and internal dialogue down to the right. When you become aware of these accessing cues you might notice some people are the

68

complete opposite. This is normal, and depends on how the question or problem faced is put to someone. This affects how the LEM behaves.

You can't just use assumption to know LEM cues; you should always make sure by testing. The simplest way to test and check is to ask a question about a feeling or a memory. For example,

What was the colour of the front door of the house you first recall living in? (V) Or, during a conversation asking them how they are feeling today. (K) A certain amount of study has been carried out on LEM. It is a fundamental lesson whilst studying NLP and very effective.

The NLP pattern and system is a generalisation and like all generalisations it isn't always perfect. The most important thing to remember is that the response will differ from person to person. So let's try a few to see where you feel your eyes move.

- Imagine a red circle inside a blue square. (V)
- When you tell yourself something good where does the voice come from? (A)
- What does it feel like to go running in the rain? (K)(V)
- What does silk feel like on the skin? (K)
- What is it like to settle into a nice warm bath at the end of the day? (K)
- What is your favourite song? (A)
- What colour is your best friend's hair? (V)

Every question will solicit a different eye movement. Now you know about this, you can make a conscious effort to be more aware of how you think and feel.

With anxiety, one of the major effects on your visual representation system is what we call negative visualisation. If you think back to the internal dialogue and look at the catastrophic mind set, then this one is critical in defeating it. You can see the event or the incident take place in front of your eyes. The colours are bright. Sometimes the picture you are visualising is static and sometimes it is moving. It may or may not have sound. Let us stop that negative visualisation picture making your anxiety ten times worse.

I want you to remember this before you start. Anything you can do in real time with a 3D object in life, you can also do with your thoughts, visions, sounds and feelings. So if I placed a dark candle in front of you now and every time you looked at it, it filled you with dread and fear, the easiest way to solve the problem would be to remove the candle. You are about to treat everything which comes your way in this chapter like that candle. So let's begin.

We will call this exercise the negative views, negative pictures. (V)

You have the picture and you can see it pretty clearly in front of your eyes. As you look and stare I want you to pay attention to the location of the picture, as later you need to take hold of it. Present thoughts generally appear directly in your line of sight. Past thoughts appear down and to the left, and future thoughts up and to the right (again this can be reversed depending on the person).

Now you have the location, I want you to answer the following:

– Is it black and white or coloured?
– Is it a still picture or is it moving?
– Does it have a border around it or just the picture?
– Is it clear or blurry?

Now you are going to ask the same questions but this time you are going to take some actions along with the questions.

Is it black and white or coloured?

OK, if it is coloured, I want you to drain the colour from it and make it black and white. If it's black and white, I want you to turn the contrast on it all the way up so all you can see is a bright, white picture in front of you.

Is it a still picture or is it moving?

If it is moving I want you to press the pause button in your mind and stop it dead.

Is it clear or blurry?

If it is clear and you can see it in full focus, I want you to distort the picture so it goes out of focus, just like the zoom on a camera or your smart phone.

Does it have a border around it or just the picture?

Now imagine one of those big, old-fashioned mirror frames. I want you to take one and place it around the circumference of the picture.

Now take the sides of the frame and fold them in towards each other, halving the picture in size and again and again, until you can comfortably grab the picture with your hand.

- Reach out and pick it up in front of you.
- Now place it over your right-hand side, out of sight from you.
- Open your eyes, take a deep breath, and when you're ready, close your eyes and see where it is.

The reason that smile starts to appear on your face is because it's no longer in your line of sight. It no longer has the emotional attachment it had. You changed its dynamics and placed it where you can't see or find it anymore. Now, with every exercise, this needs your undivided focus and attention and repetition here is the key. You do get to have control over every thought and feeling you have. You get to decide if you pay it attention or you simply detach from it, play around with it, and remove the attachment to it.

You can do so much more with this. You can add questions. You can make them more detailed. But I don't want to over-complicate the methods I am showing you at this stage. This book is written for you and you only need the fundamentals to make a massive impact straight away in your battle with anxiety. So my question now would be, how does that feel?

Now you have mastered the visual part, let's look at the audio part. We all have our own internal dialogue – the words we use for self-talk – and we know how important it is and how vital that the right words are said. But sometimes, when anxiety creeps in, you have another version of self-talk happening. It can be difficult to stop this when the anxiety starts or the self-doubt creeps in. We call this the good angel vs the bad devil. It's almost as if there are two people on your shoulders giving you advice and harmful dialogue at the same time. The good angel part you don't need to alter or interfere with, as it's good with a good intent. The bad, however, needs to be removed and not listened to in any way, shape or form. If a song or a TV show is playing that you don't like, what's the simplest way to stop it affecting you? Simple, mute it or turn down the volume. It's that basic principle you are going to work with now, and you call this exercise 'a quiet mind'. (A)

And so it starts, and you hear that negative voice in your head with the repeated message, or the catastrophizing thought with words on a loop.

Close your eyes and pay attention to every word, and the rhythm, speed and volume it is being delivered in.

Taking the thumb and forefinger on either hand, use that as your volume control.

This control changes the volume, and when pressed, the volume button will appear in front of your eyes.

Concentrate and bring it down a step with every press; I want you to focus and press in and turn it from a 10 to a 9.

Now 8, 7, 6, 5, 4, 3, 2, 1, Mute.

As you get to mute, notice the number change from a number to a small speaker with a line running through it, just like it does on your TV.

Now take a breath and close your eyes again and notice the sounds. If they are gone that's perfect. If they are still there but a lot quieter then close your eyes and let's repeat the exercise until they are gone. Once they are gone, I have a question:

What does it finally feel like to have peace and quiet in your mind for the first time in a long time?

You have played around and adjusted pictures and sounds that can cause or appear with the anxiety. Now you will look at the third stage. Feelings. As you know, these are so important in your life and the words = thoughts, thoughts = feelings can now be taken one step further. Feelings = actions and outcomes. You base all your actions on the feelings you get at the time. If you carry out a task or do something that has a negative effect, you tend to remember that fairly clearly. So when it comes to repeating that task, you hold off because you know the feeling it involves is that of a negative state. But what happens when anxiety is inside and you don't get it at stage one – the inkling? That results in the heavy, swirly, dark, cloudy feeling in your chest or stomach that feels so heavy and damaging. It pretty much stops you in your tracks. But now I get to show you exactly how to control and remove that feeling.

We call this from the inside out. (K)

First I want you to focus on that feeling and scale it from 1-10. You follow a very similar process to the visual removal. You ask the following questions of that feeling, but before you do, I want you to imagine that you can turn your eyes all the way down and look down on it from above.

Does the feeling have any colour? Does the felling have a sound to it? Is it static or moving?

Is it clear or blurry?

Are you looking at it or out from it?

Does it have a frame or border around it? Does it have any shape to it?

Once you have the answers, you can change the feeling. And remember what I said earlier – any 3D object that you can hold in your hand and change, you can also do with a feeling. So with that in mind, you now do the following:

Does the feeling have any colour?

Drain any colour from the feeling and make it white. Once it is white, turn up the contrast and make the white as bright as you can – almost like a neon bulb.

Does the felling have a sound to it?

Do exactly the same to the sound as you would do a sound in your head – turn it down and mute it using the same process.

Is it static or moving?

If it is moving, either like a wave from side to side, or circular, or clouds of smoke, then use the thumb and forefinger and pause the movement until it is perfectly still.

Is it clear or blurry?

If it is crystal clear, change the focus until it is blurry.

Are you looking at it or out from it?

If you are looking out from it, imagine standing above and look down on it.

Does it have a frame or border around it?

If not, again you put a frame or border around the entire shape that you see.

Now take the edge of the frame and fold it in half, and again and again, until it is no more than the size of a stamp.

And now you have two options:

Option one. Focus on it and move it from inside to outside. Follow it all the way out until it sits about six inches from you.

Now take a deep breath and blow on it, and push it further and further away, until it drops off the edge of the horizon you can see.

Option two. Take a large gulp, and as you swallow, imagine that gulp going all the way down, until it hits the top of the frame and dislodges it from its location. Then let gravity do its job and follow it all the way down through the body; into the legs and out of the feet until it sits outside, just in front of the foot. Now flick your foot up and touch the edge of the frame and watch it move further and further away again until it disappears over the horizon.

Open your eyes, take a really deep breath and then close your eyes and see where that feeling has gone. Again, if you have just reduced it, you repeat it until you can scale from 1-3 at a comfortable level.

Negative thoughts always come with a feeling, and if you can beat the feeling you can beat the thought. This process is all about reprograming your habitual instinctive behaviours and doing things differently. It is the easy option to give in to these words, thoughts and feelings. You are not the kind of person to let them beat you, hold you down and control your life. How do I know? Because you are on a quest for answers, for different methods and techniques to beat and overcome the anxiety which controls you. That's exactly why I know you won't be giving in without a fight.

And, in case no one has mentioned this to you today, I will. For that, once again, well done. Desire and inner fight is a fine quality to exhibit, and you're doing exactly that. You must feel so proud that you haven't just laid down and let it control you.

8

Universal Energy:
The Power of Inner Healing

You have doubtless gathered by now that the person healing your anxiety is you. No? Think about energy for a moment. Universal energy. Take what psychoanalyst Carl Jung called the 'collective unconscious' a step further. Let's explore that for a bit.

You might think the idea of having an aura is a bit 'out-there', but what if you called the aura an energy-field? Energy is around us and within us but normally unavailable to the five senses. You can't see, hear, smell, taste or touch it…but you can feel it.

Still don't believe me? Think of a time when you have been in a room by yourself, perhaps looking out of a window, daydreaming, reading a book etc. and someone else walks into the room behind you and doesn't make a sound. They approach slowly and then, (unless you are fully submerged in your subconscious i.e. totally absorbed in a book) you suddenly become aware of them. You sense their presence. You use this phrase a lot without really thinking about what it means, their energy-fields meet yours, and you know they are behind you. This is the subconscious alerting you to another's presence, one of the many jobs it can do for you, and it works best when you are relaxed and aware of it.

Universal energy can be seen, with a bit of practise, when there are no artificial lights, or in low-lighting, and also behind your closed eyelids. Energy appears as coloured mists in the hues of the spectrum: red, orange, yellow, green, blue, indigo and violet. Fused together, they become white. Next time you see a rainbow, you'll have a jolt of recognition – those are your energy colours appearing across the sky; the same ones connecting you to your subconscious.

And now I will show you a way to connect with universal energy as part of your self-healing process. Once again, practise... and have fun.

A quick exercise to connect with your energy centre:

1. Sit somewhere quiet and peaceful. Close your eyes and take a few deep breaths.
2. Your focus will now be behind your eyelids. Move that focus down to your core, the centre of your body, your abdomen, the area where you sometimes get 'gut feelings' about people, places and situations which can't be explained using the five senses. (To help this along, you might imagine that you have stomach-ache and focus on that area.) This area is your energy centre.
3. Now imagine a ball of white energy spinning around in your energy centre. Feel it pulsing in and out of your body as it spins. Know that this is your own personal energy and you are in control of it. Do this any time you have a quiet moment and the more often you practise the easier it will be to connect, until you can do it instantly.
4. Imagine the colours of the spectrum – red, orange, yellow, green, blue, indigo, violet – and see them floating around you in mists. Starting with red, picture the colour and feel it pulsing into your energy centre. Then picture orange, yellow etc. Feel every colour pulsing into this white ball of energy and know it is growing stronger and you are growing stronger with it. See and feel all the colours fusing together and the ball pulsing pure energy in and around you.
5. When you are feeling anxious, this ball of energy will probably be spinning like a Catherine Wheel. So, focus on the white ball and slow it down. Take control. Feel it slowing and yourself relaxing, as it becomes a gentle, pulsing rhythm deep within you.
6. When you feel relaxed and calm, move your focus back up through your body to the space behind your eyelids. Do you see any coloured mist here? If so, note the colour and just watch it for a bit. You've connected with one of

your energy colours. Give yourself a quick, imaginary pat on the back and allow yourself to feel excited. You are well on the way to self-healing.

7. When you feel ready, blink your eyes a few times, then open them. You may feel a bit disorientated the first few times you try this, but don't panic, this is normal as you return to the room. The more you practise this, the more you'll enjoy it. Think of it as your own personal control-centre.

Now you are in command. Anxiety – watch out. Chakras

Chakra is a Sanskrit word which means 'wheel' and the colours of the spectrum relate to energy points throughout the body. Once you start working with your energy centre, as in the exercise above, and seeing these colours behind your eyelids, you may want to learn more about each colour and the meaning behind it.

Below is a beginner's guide to the seven centres and their corresponding colours.

The crown chakra is a beautiful colour to see. If you focus behind your eyelids and see a violet mist then know that this is healing and send it through your body. Feel it flow down and pulse out and join the white ball of energy, then slow this down to a relaxing pace and simply focus on it for as long as it takes to feel calm.

Now you're going to focus on the technique you learned earlier in the book, visualisation. But you will take this a step further and amplify it big time.

Visualisation = imagination + feeling.

When you use your imagination to visualise a scene in which you are taking part, it is very important to use it the correct way. Let's take an example,

You have to give a speech/talk in public. This could be a wedding, after-dinner speech, a presentation at work or a prize-giving etc. I'll use a speech on a stage in front of an audience for this exercise and give two scenarios.

1. In your imagination, when you visualise yourself giving this speech, do you see your whole body on the stage, as if you are watching a film in which you are starring? If so, then you have made a common mistake. This separates you from the action and stops the subconscious from doing its work.
2. Instead, in your imagination, feel the stage beneath your feet. Look down and see your shoes, your hands leaning on the lectern. Look ahead and see the faces of the audience staring at you. This is the correct way to visualise if you want to effect change you are always inside your own body, looking through your eyes.

Practise the second example for a few moments and feel yourself on the stage. What happens when you look down at the audience and see those faces staring back at you? Anxiety? Take a moment to examine this feeling and see how strong it is.

At this point you are going to use something called the Law of Assumption.

This is great fun to do and can have incredibly positive effects on you and the way you feel about events, people and situations in your life. What the law states is: 'What you assume to be true, will become your reality.' If this is the case, then why not assume a really positive reality for yourself? Test it out. See what happens. Again, have fun.

If you go back to the speech example, and the visualisation where you feel yourself standing on the stage facing the audience, you will now add a crucial element. The key to success. Feeling.

How would you feel if you have given this speech and it's been successful? What would be the best possible end result for you in this scenario? Note I said 'end result' – not the speech itself. If you start to imagine actually giving the speech then you lay yourself open to countless forms of anxiety; i.e. what if I'm speaking too fast? What exactly am I saying? Have I slurred any words? Am I loud enough – can everyone at the back hear me? Etc.

Instead, imagine the speech is over. The best possible end result. Close your eyes, fire up your imagination and try this:

You are walking off the stage. Feel the wood beneath your feet as you descend the steps. Hear tumultuous applause all around you. See someone approach (an organiser/someone you know) they tell you, "Well done," "Fantastic speech," and shake your hand. Feel their hand in yours. Smile at them. Think to yourself, 'I've done it. Wow, this feels good.' Use your five senses. Maybe someone else hands you a bouquet of flowers and they smell gorgeous. You feel fantastic. Relieved. Elated. Appreciated. You gave the best speech ever.

Keep it short, sweet and full of feeling. Repeat this over and over any chance you get to relax and close your eyes. The feeling is the most important part, the magic happens when you feel this as real, it's already happened. And, of course, write your speech, practise it, try it out on someone you trust, do the usual things you would – but keep your 'best speech' ending in your head every chance you get. See what happens.

You can use this technique for any situation where anxiety rears its ugly head. Simply ask yourself, how would I feel if I got the outcome I want? The best possible end result? And go straight there in your head – with feeling.

Remember you are healing yourself, and you're doing a bloody good job.

9

FEAR = Face
Everything and Rise

One word goes hand in hand with the other: anxiety and fear. One often follows the other and is never far behind. It could be a million and one things which brought anxiety to your door – past, present, or even future thoughts actions and concerns but one thing is for sure: fear will always be attached to it.

I work very hard to help eradicate anxiety for my clients and anyone I deal with, and over the past few months I have noted that it isn't just anxiety which is hurting people, it's also the fear which goes with it. Often you can deal with anxiety if it was just that alone, but when you put fear beside anxiety as a pair then it becomes a bigger battle; a battle which can seem hopeless and overwhelming. I promise you that feeling is simply your thoughts messing with you. During this part, you will rely on facts over thoughts, and show you how to 'Face Everything and Rise'. I will show you ways of dealing with the initial thoughts and easing the worry and anxiety which is so destructive to your way of life.

Always play the FACT vs THOUGHT game: Here is the initial thought or worry. It starts to creep up on you. You can feel it. You can see it coming and until now you couldn't do much about it.

Let's change that.

As the thought or feeling starts to creep up on you, in your loudest voice (in your own mind) scream 'STOP.' That will stop all thoughts and feelings dead for a few seconds and allow you the clarity to self-analyse. Now you look at what you are about to worry about or become scared of, and you place it out in front of us and you pin it to a wall. Then, you look at the facts and place them next to the worry/fear.

So, for example, thought: You have applied for a new position and a total job change. The expected response time is between ten and fourteen days. Day fourteen comes and goes and you hear nothing back. Straight away your negative anxious side takes you to, 'Oh, I haven't got it, they haven't replied and I am going to be stuck without a position for the rest of my life, I have no money no job and the future is bleak I don't even know why I bother sometimes.'

Fact; you failed to read the response time accurately and it says approximately ten to fourteen days depending on bank holidays and if received on a weekend it may be longer. It may actually be en route to you now and you can't jump straight to the worst possibility.

To resolve this, you either make a follow up call or email to ask if they received your application. Remember the importance of clear communications in life. The easiest way to solve a problem is by clear lines of communication. Instead of going straight for the negative response, look at it factually and do a follow up to get the answer you are looking for.

Be strong, be focused: I receive so many calls and messages from clients who have so much positivity and value to offer, if they could only remain strong and focussed. You become what you think. If you wake and the first thing you do is give yourself a blast of negative self-talk then that's the mood for the rest of the day. Trust me when I say anxiety is not hard-wired into your brain forever. It is a thought process and a way of thinking which was developed by you at some stage, and with any pattern or habit, it can and it will be broken. Just because you are struggling now doesn't mean it will be this way forever: it won't. It can and it will be changed. But for that to happen, you need to want to change it, to wake up and fight, drive and focus on beating this every single day. The more positive and focused on beating anxiety you are, the easier it is to beat it in the long run.

What really is fear: It is a thought, an emotion, a perception, a self-destructive pattern of thinking. It is also what keeps you on your toes and gives you, at times, a razor sharp focus. Fear is not just a negative emotion, it is also positive and you just need to learn how to use it to your advantage instead of against you. OK, so you ask, how do you do that? Well, you simply use it to drive you and to remind yourself that you are a normal, healthy, walking, talking human being. You need all these emotions in life to keep you focused and driven when you need to.

Fear isn't something which always has to be a negative in life. In fact, you can use it to enhance your performance and your perceptions of how and why you do things. Use fear as a motivator. Use it to go as hard as you can at every task which scares you and everything you are afraid of. Use fear as a positive and it will push you harder than normal intrinsic motivation ever could. Let's look at people with extremely high-risk jobs: oil rig workers, pilots, armed forces, law enforcement – all these jobs have an extremely high-risk factor to them. If the people who carried them out hid from the reality and the fear which comes with them, well, there wouldn't be anyone in that field. In fact, they use the fear of failure to keep them focused, driven and giving it everything they have.

Share/talk/mind map: If you have so many thoughts, fears and anxieties which make you feel as though you can't breathe at times, keeping them all to yourself is doing more damage than good. Acid will do more damage to the container it is carried in than the object it is poured over. That may seem like one of those good old sayings people like to bandy about and post on social media, but it is very true. You need an outlet. You need someone to share with. You have to have a way of letting it out and allowing someone to hear it, maybe to offer some advice or even just to be there and listen.

Even if you have no one, get a pen and paper and list the worry/fear/problem. Get it out onto the paper and then sit back and look at it as if you were a friend about to offer advice. Reach out to the local GP, and if they aren't helpful and just feel the need to put you on medication, then go private and reach out to a therapist, life coach, or any other organisation which can guide you and offer you valuable guidance. Mind mapping is another way of dealing with your thoughts and fears. Start at the centre and work outward; you will be amazed at the progress you can make just by having your fears and anxieties laid out in front of you in black and white.

Make decisions on outcomes, not emotions (ecology checks): Here's a quick example; a lady and gentleman meet at a party, they click, hit it off straight away and there is a ton of sexual chemistry involved. They spend the night together and, from that moment on, seem hooked. They start to lose friends and social circles and everything they do revolves around each other. After only a few short weeks, they both decide that it would be a great idea to move in together, and then, after less than a month, they have moved in, are expecting a child, and reality hits home: things don't seem so bright after all.

Finances are now brought into the equation; friends, family and, of course, schedules and life commitments. Perhaps one or both have had children previously, and, in the whirlwind of the romance, failed to mention it. Before long, one person feels trapped and the cracks start to show. The relationship ends and a lot of issues need to be faced. That choice was based on the emotion of the moment, the lust, the excitement, the whirlwind romance they perceived to be in. Everything was based on a good feeling at the time (an emotion).

Now, I am an advocate of love at first sight and do genuinely think that when that situation happens, you don't need to look at the second part. There is something so beautiful and magical about meeting your soulmate and I believe that we all have one. The situation described, we shall say, is not that. If either party had paused looked at the situation and ecology and checked the choices they were about to make, I think you would have had a very different outcome.

It's the same when a relationship breaks up. We tend to do the ecology check in that instance, hence the choice made was based on fact and outcome not feeling. An ecology check is akin to dropping a pebble in a pond. It will cause ripples. Some will be fairly small but some will be bigger – we call these the negative and positive effects of the choice. And for this choice the question or action in question is:

Do I fight this anxiety or do I just accept this is how I am?

Let's take the second part of that question and ecology check it first.

Do I just accept this is how I am?

Negative	Positive
Anxiety stays Sadness Worry No lifestyle change Pain Reclusive Worried Physical symptoms may increase Lack confidence Lack self-esteem Withdrawn Work affected May lose friends/family/loved ones Condition myself to anxiety No control No drive No determination (this list can be endless in relation to negative effect on your life)	Familiarity Excuse my behaviours in my own mind

You then look at the negative and positive effects of accepting that choice and in this case, the negative outweigh the positive ten-fold. Straight away, if this question is looked at factually and not emotionally, it screams the answer to you. Although the answer also needs the same process, you will notice a big difference.

Do I fight this anxiety?

Negative	Positive
Effort Change my routine Uncertainty	Anxiety-free Power of my choices Confidence Lifestyle changes Control over emotions Happiness Freedom Improved family life Less stress No panic attacks No worries Sense of achievement Sense of direction Sense of accomplishment Finding my inner fight Inner desire Will power increases Clear head Quiet mind Peacefulness Calm inside No physical symptoms to affect me Freedom of choice

The major difference here is clear to see. If you choose the first part of the question and you look at it factually, you have so much more to gain. Once you have the question and you have the positive and negative effects in life, you now need to include how these choices will affect the people in your life. As a starting point, you look at it and look at the negative and positive effects on those people. Let's take family as the first group. You now ask, 'If I was to make the choice I have chosen above, how would it effect the people in my inner circle?'

How will this affect my family?	
Negative	**Positive**
	Opens up a new way of life anxiety free
	Less worried about my mental health
	More activities open to us
	Less stress
	Better family environment
	Better communication all round
	Positive role model setting (shows inner strength)
	Lead by example
	Less worry
	Happiness
	Pride
	No more walking on eggshells depending on mood

I can't think of any negative effects becoming anxiety-free would have on family life, so I have left that one blank. You then go on to repeat the process. It can be looked at with relationships, work, social life and any other area which this choice will affect. Once you have all the positive and negative effects of the choice you are going to make, you lay them out in front of us and you ask one simple question.

Are you prepared and willing to accept and overcome all negative effects and ripples in order to have positive ones back in your life?

If the answer is yes, then you have just made your first choice using an ecology check based on facts and outcomes and not emotional states.

Now you have made a choice and that should feel pretty good and empowering. You are starting to take control and make choices based on the facts and the outcomes. This ecology check can be used for all areas in life such as a career change, relationship change, job opportunities, financial investments, life choices etc. It removes the fear and worry about making split second choices based on a fleeting emotion. Now the choice is made, you go to the very next phase of your ecology check and that is another question.

What actions do I need to take to achieve the end state – in this case, it is anxiety free?

Again, you look at the end state as the destination. For us to reach that destination you need to go on a journey and this part is what doors do – you need to go through them to get from A to B.

Learn and understand what anxiety is (knowledge is power).
Learn methods and techniques to control and diminish it.
Self-help books.
Therapist.
Practice.
Inner healing methods.
Try different methods.
Talk with fellow sufferers and gain insight how they beat anxiety.

Join different social media groups such as 'anxiety-free' as they also have a wealth of knowledge.

Once you have the doors you need to open, you take each one in turn, open it and walk right through. You are one step closer to becoming anxiety-free. You might just be surprised at how much you already know and just how well prepared you are for an anxiety-free life. Remember, you are doing things differently now, you are fighting on a whole new level, and you must approach each day with the qualities needed to beat anxiety.

I use an acronym called CMADE:

Confidence: Again, this has been fairly knocked with anxiety and it is key. I don't mean you have to walk about showing the world how confident you are pretending to be. I mean confidence in your own ability to beat this. You are more powerful and beautiful than an emotion.

Manner: When you use that all important dialogue, talk to yourself with pride, passion and empowerment. You wouldn't believe anyone standing in front of you who was whimpering and sounding doubtful, so don't use that manner on yourself.

Attitude: You have made a choice, and a start, so remember that you can and will beat this. Go into it with a winning attitude. Don't have self-doubt or worry. Start each day as you mean to end it and do it with a swagger and sense of self-pride. Get the attitude part correct and the others will follow.

Diligence: Give this your all and give it every day. Practise, read, practise and practise some more – you can't drive a car perfectly without taking lessons first. This is the lessons part; practise with everything you have, and when the day is done, I would like you to sit on your bed and ask the following question: 'Today, did I give my all in the fight with anxiety?' If the answer is 'yes' – well done and be proud. If not, then don't expect to be driving a car before you can answer yes to the last question.

Enthusiasm: How many times have you heard the saying, 'Their enthusiasm was contagious?' Well, that's exactly what I want you to do. Look at the end goal, close your eyes and see yourself anxiety-free, living the life you want and not being controlled by emotion. Really look at it. That is all you need to become enthusiastic about this journey.

10

Happiness by Change Not Chance

As you already know, now you are not leaving anything to chance. You are changing what you do and going again but going at it differently. If you try it differently you will then have a different outcome. But one of the key elements is commitment to change, and it's easy to say you want to do something. That's what New Year's resolutions are based on; change and doing things differently. But over 80% of people who start something new or try something different falter in a few short days or weeks. Then they decide they will get started tomorrow. Probably.

You rely solely on willpower to make this happen. If you think back to the start of the book, you will remember willpower is stored in the conscious mind and is about ten percent of the power of your mind. Hence ten versus a ninety percent behaviour takes much more than willpower to change it. Having said that, at times willpower can be an amazing adversary; look at all the therapies and groups that reply solely on it, such as AA, GA, DV groups, to talk and use willpower to change a behaviour.

The difference between those types of groups and normal use of willpower is that each one has committed fully to that change, and that involves more than just a word and a statement saying 'I will change and do more and do better.' Every change you encounter will usually have an element of fear and possible short-term pain involved. That's the main reason people don't follow through or commit to the change. They are scared of the short-term pain.

Let's look at a smoker, for example. If they go into change with a limiting belief that stopping smoking will be too hard for them, or they aren't capable of achieving the end goal, then the battle is lost before it begins. They know the short-term pain of the craving is going to hurt them and even more so if they don't think it's going to work. Why put yourself through short-term pain in the beginning for it not to work?

In order for you to change and become better, you have to accept that to achieve long-term happiness you may have to take some short-term pain. But it is only short-term. With anxiety, it may be the short-term pain of fighting your thoughts, feelings, and emotions full on every day for a few days, weeks, or months. It might be the uncomfortable social circles you have to put yourself in, or the stark reality that you have a fight on your hands. So, how do you commit to change? Well, you have a few things you need to look at and they all start with you

Challenge and alter your expectations: So far your expectations haven't really amounted to much and anxiety has a major role to play in that. But I am not interested in having you look at today in this respect. I am talking future expectations. I am talking about when you live an anxiety-free life and what your expectations are and I am sure they will be extremely high. If you think big and have great expectations then you achieve big. Let's look at Steve Jobs. He created Apple, the largest tech company in the world. Did you know that he dropped out of college after only one term to go back-packing around the world, and never finished his education there? Despite taking an annual salary of one USD his net worth was 8.3 billion when he passed in 2011. His expectations for himself and his future are exactly what I am talking about.

Don't be afraid of failure: Even the word sounds harsh and alters your expectations if it is used too much. Failure is such a horrible term, and from now on you don't get to use it. It has too many negative connotations and stirs automatic self-critical thoughts about yourself, so you simply change that one word. You change it to 'EL' – enhanced learning. Everything you do can be used for enhanced learning and some of the lessons taught are extremely valuable in life.

All you have to do is sit down and look at what happened. I don't mean relive every single second of the EL; I mean look at the parts which affected the outcome. Was it something a third party did? Was it something you did? Was it within your control or out of control? Once you get those parts, you ask what lesson can I take, and if I were to do the same event again, what would I change to get a different, better outcome? EL is to be embraced, and if you are going to get it wrong, go big or go home, because you can always take so much from it. If you look at some of the top businessmen and leaders in the world, past and present, they all have one common trait. They never use the word 'fail' and they took something from every EL situation and became bigger and better than ever before. So the message is simple: don't be scared or worried about it, just revisit and learn that lesson.

If at first you don't succeed, try a different way: We have all heard of the saying, 'If at first you don't succeed; try, try again.' Let's not use that anymore. The simple fact remains that if you didn't manage it the first time you tried, you won't on the second or third. You become tired. Remember, the mind and body are directly linked at every level, and if you couldn't get over the six-foot wall on the first attempt, then you are going to be more drained and tired the second and third time. Emotionally, it is no different. If you have tried to beat anxiety one way and it hasn't worked, then stop trying the same way. Change the behaviour or the method and again you change the outcome.

If you have put the advice from the previous chapters into practise, this part makes perfect sense. If the objective is to get to the other side of the wall and you can't get over it, why not try going round, under, or through it? The whole point of buying and reading this book is that you are already doing something different, so let's keep the momentum going. Let's try different things in the battle with anxiety. Unless you defeat it and replace it, you won't ever be free from it.

Create your trigger list: Anxiety – depending on its state and representation in your life – will often come and go. Sometimes it will come out of nowhere, and other times you can trigger it via certain environmental traits. A smell, a song, a location, an activity or an event can trigger anxiety. List the triggers that cause you anxiety. Really think about these. You are going to be working on them soon.

For now, you will avoid these situations until you are ready to face them full on. The reason for facing them is to show you that you can live a normal life. Any location, event or whoever you are surrounded by do not cause anxiety. It's not the situation which makes you anxious. The emotional attachment you have to it triggers the anxiety. You can't live life avoiding certain things, people or situations. If that were so, the anxiety would still have control over your actions. So you make a list of the things that you know and later you will have all the control in the world to tackle them. But, for now, you are doing things differently. You are beating and taking control of the anxiety. You need to give yourself some breathing space to put everything you have learned into practise.

Start listening to your gut feeling: We all have it; that little tingle or uncertain feeling in your stomach when a new situation, person, or offer arrives. How many times has something happened and your gut feeling said it wasn't a good idea but you went ahead with it anyway – only for that initial feeling to be correct? It's the same in the battle with anxiety. If you don't think it is for you and think it may make matters worse, trust your gut feeling. Instead of making a choice on the spot, if possible, go straight to an ecology check. Ecology checks can be completed inside your own mind for instances like this. When practiced and given everything, you can do them in a few minutes inside your head. You can save yourself days, weeks and, in some cases, months of hurt and pain. Don't risk increasing your anxiety for the sake of a few moments looking at everything factually and not emotionally. Remember, happiness by change not chance.

Train at every waking moment: Let's look at professional athletes. Are they born superhuman at their chosen field or sport? No, they live, breathe and train hard every day to become the best. Think of your task here as a sport, and the sport is called Anxiety Freedom. You need to immerse yourself in the methods and techniques which will make you a winner, and give it everything you have at every spare moment. You start the day on a positive. You have affirmations. You eat healthily, you exercise and you practice your new methods on a daily basis until it becomes muscle memory and an instant reaction.

You look to the future with positive visualisation. Look at sprint runners for example when they are lined up, they don't even blink. They have a focus and determination in their eye as they look up at the track. They are visualising the end result; themselves crossing the line. Not everyone will finish in first place on that event, but they do all finish. To be an athlete on that stage in the first place is all part of their dream. It's what they have trained and practiced for all their life and it shows.

We all have excuses for why we don't have time during the day to train and practice the things I have shown you. But, in this case, it is black and white. Do you want the change? Then you have to behave and do things differently. If it means setting an alarm to get up 10-15 mins early, so you can have some quiet visualisation ready for the day ahead, then that's what you do. If you can't sleep because the anxiety doesn't seem to let us, then you get proactive. You are awake anyway, so instead of just feeling aggrieved by it, you pick up the book, you take an exercise and you read and practice. You read and practice until it becomes second nature. You do things differently and you get different results, but you have to commit to the change. You have to know one hundred percent that it is going to work and it will change your life.

Focus on the "Whats", Not the "What Ifs": We have already looked at the different types of internal dialogue. The common trait with all of them is that we tend to live in the future and try to predict what is coming. The future hasn't arrived yet, so there's no possible way of knowing what will be in a week, month or even a year. The exception is that you can predict you will be anxiety free. That is the one key element which I want you to look at when your mind starts getting ahead of yourself. But for now, you can spend hours worrying, triggering your anxiety and building it up into this massive beast which won't allow you to live – but what's the point? That isn't going to change anything. All you have is the present moment and time. That's why it's called the 'present' because, if looked at and embraced, it really can be a gift. Look at the things you have right now which are good, strong, or positive. Be precise here and list them down. We all have one thing to be thankful and grateful for. I will start you off and you can add to it.

1. Desire to understand my anxiety.
2. Taking the first step by learning more.
3. Trying new methods and techniques to beat and control my anxiety.

Now you have a list of positive things you have, or qualities about yourself. Really look at it; things like kindness, honesty, and empathy are all beautiful and powerful traits in a person. These are often missed or over-looked when anxiety comes into your life. Remember, anxiety is just a behaviour and emotion which has been set out on a subconscious level with a positive intention. It's the behaviour which has gone out of sync with the intention.

Now you see the qualities you have for the first time in a long time. Look and acknowledge each and one. Just like you, they are truly remarkable. All you have is the present moment, and that's where your energy and focus needs to be. Only by focusing on the positive do you get to see it. So far you have allowed yourself to focus on the negative and that's not working out too good. Again, I sound like a broken record. Happiness by change not chance.

Go and stand in front of the mirror again. Look at yourself before you read on. Smile, give yourself thanks for getting this far into the book, not giving up, and trying all the different methods and techniques I have shown you. Notice any change in yourself. You will, for the first time, be looking at yourself through a different set of eyes. You will look with compassion, understanding and with the knowledge that you are doing something to beat and remove anxiety like never before. For that, tell yourself 'thank you' and just look. It's OK to get emotional. It's OK to have tears right now. It's OK to feel lighter and slightly different in your relationship with anxiety.

It's OK to love yourself for the first time in a long time. For that, I admire you. What you're seeing right now for the first time is something very beautiful and strong.

Now see and feel the change: I am going to take you back to the 'old school' ways. Again, you have a million resources available to you. There are a million different ways to get to the destination. But for us to see it working and feel it working, that intrinsic motivation to keep pushing on will push us harder and faster than before. So how do you gauge exactly how this journey is going for you? Well, that's the easy part. I want you to keep an anxiety log. Keep a small writing pad at the side of your bed. Before you retire for the day, write down your anxiety level. I will keep it simple for now: 1-10, with 1 being no real anxiety and 10 being uppermost on the scale. Then make a brief summary of the day and list the things you did differently. If any particular thing worked, put a little asterisk beside it.

If something works well, you will include it in your daily routine. If something sets you off, you do the same and avoid it until you are in a position to tackle it. The whole point of this lesson is that you get to track your anxiety levels. There is no one better qualified than you to do this. If, after a few days or a week, you have a noticeable pattern, then go into the next week using that as a basis for your actions and behaviours. You are learning what is working and tracking it and you are learning what is not working and you are tracking that. Again, think back to when we talked about EL opportunities. Now you are putting that principle into practice, and learning everything you need to structure and plan the week ahead.

Allow a wobble: Not everyone who has climbed Everest made it on the first attempt. Many tried, failed and tried again. They learned the lesson and embraced the EL opportunities they gained on the first attempt, re-organised and tried again. Your battle with anxiety is the same. The one key element here is that early on you got your mind-set correct and you made a choice. You looked at the positive and negative effects of your choice and you decided to go for it. This in itself can cause a bit of anxiety and that's perfectly fine. Anxiety is a normal emotion which should come and go like other feelings. If you do feel a bit of anxiety at the lifestyle and emotional changes you are going to make, then that's OK.

Remember, there is a massive difference between a normal touch of anxiety and having it controlling your life and sculpting your future. To have a setback early on is OK. Think of it this way – when you learned to ride a bike, the first time you fell off, did you just give up and never try again? Or a driving test, or a maths exam? No, you learned which part was wrong, corrected it and tried again. This is the exact same learning model you use when it comes to anxiety and learning to control and defeat it. The consistency has to be the same. You have to understand that every single method or technique may not work first time, every time, but you will improve and get stronger the more you work at it. Another downside to anxiety is the whole self-critical approach you take on without thinking. Well, that was before and this is now. If you wobble along the way, accept it. Don't be disheartened. Learn from it, look at your actions and see where you can tweak and improve. Then go again.

Option 2 always: Think back to the two options you had when you looked at how you would treat others. Today, wake and remind yourself that you are now, and always will be, treating yourself like option 2. Option 2 is the way of compassion, understanding, love, acceptance, empathy and beauty. At the end of it, you have something too beautiful and bright for anything to extinguish the flame burning inside us. For you to treat yourself differently would result in heightened anxiety. That crippling emotion would not fade away. You would be living as if you were on a hamster wheel, going round and round. And then you get so tired and drained you give up and accept the unacceptable.

With option 2, it opens us up to whole new world of possibilities and changes. So you take option 2 and you go at it differently

See anxiety in a different light: Up until now, we have looked on anxiety with contempt and as something which has hurt, damaged and constrained us. But we are not looking closely enough. We are only seeing it through an emotional and feeling perspective. Anxiety has come into your life for a reason. At times, you can take away some positives – we call these anxiety super powers. People with anxiety often show certain qualities and traits which people without anxiety have to learn and adapt to. Having anxiety increases your sense of the world and the environmental situations around you. Super powers don't mean that you can walk on water but it does mean that you are a lot more in tune with the world than you think.

Ability to sense and feel the energy around us: This is one of the more powerful super powers. Anxious people are more capable of seeing and feeling negative people and situations that go on, in and around us. They can sense if someone is negative and pulling their energy down. This is why some people with anxiety can be classed as rude. That's not the case. They just don't want to interact with negative people or situations.

Heightened empathy: One of the most beautiful, amazing qualities which people have is empathy. Unfortunately, this can't be taught in a class or from a text book. Lots of people suffer from lack of empathy. Being touched by or understanding someone's problems and situations and wanting to help, even though you may be struggling yourself, is something so bright and beautiful it should be worshiped and celebrated. You have something very special. That makes you very special.

Heightened emotional intelligence: Anxiety sufferers spend so much time analysing, thinking and playing out events and situations in their own mind. Studies have suggested that, because of these traits, people who suffer anxiety in general have a higher IQ than those who don't.

Internal lie detector: As well as feeling negativity around us and spending so much time analysing everything, you have become allergic to fabrication. If lies are told, people with anxiety will pick up on them very quickly and challenge the lie. They will look at it and make sure it sits right with them, before accepting it as fact. This is one of the main reasons people who tend to stretch the truth do not like being around people with anxiety. Liars will use that as an excuse to stay away or not interact with you. They take their problem and try and spin it and put the emphasis on you. They announce that you are rude or abrupt. But you can see through lies, and they don't want to be challenged. Instead of dealing with their issue, they project onto you.

Many of the anxiety sufferers who come to me for help don't see the super powers, despite knowing they are there. Once again, you fall into the trap of letting that one powerful emotion change the light on everything you look at. You let anxiety distort the facts into feelings and have us look at everything from an emotional stand point.

Try a therapist: In my battle with anxiety, one of the most profound factors in overcoming it was going into therapy. I already understood NLP and I chose NLP and Hypnotherapy therapy. I wasn't gaining much by visiting someone each week and talking and re-living all the different memories and emotional triggers that sent me back to living with anxiety. I already knew how very powerful NLP was for me. Therapy is an amazing tool to help deal with and beat anxiety once and for all. I will give you a few different options to look at and see what one works best for you.

NLP: The methods and techniques I use in this book are predominately NLP based and focused. This type of therapy is based on actions as opposed to the words. It works on making the change and gives you the tools to let you alter and re-evaluate your emotional state. It helps you relook your situation and push yourself to the limits.

CBT: Cognitive Behavioural Therapy. This is a talking therapy. It has been proven to help treat a wide range of emotional and physical health conditions in adults, young people and children. CBT looks at how you think about a situation and how this affects the way you act.

EFT/Tapping: EFT provides relief from chronic pain, emotional problems, disorders, addictions, phobias, post-traumatic stress disorder and physical diseases. Like acupuncture and acupressure, tapping is a set of techniques which utilise the body's energy meridian points.

EMDR: Eye movement desensitisation and reprocessing is a form of psychotherapy developed by Francine Shapiro. It uses eye movements or other forms of bilateral stimulation to assist trauma victims in processing distressing memories and beliefs.

Hypnotherapy: Hypnotherapy is a type of complementary and alternative medicine. The mind is used to help with a variety of problems, such as breaking bad habits or coping with stress.

Psychotherapy: Psychotherapy is the use of psychological methods, particularly when based on regular personal interaction. This helps someone change and overcome problems in desired ways

Applied relaxation therapy: This involves learning how to relax your muscles in situations where you normally experience anxiety.

Art therapy: A form of psychotherapy involving the encouragement of free self-expression through painting, drawing, or modelling. This is used as a remedial or diagnostic activity.

All of these therapies are available privately. A good starting point would be to google local therapy in your area. Any therapist worth their salt will be happy to chat on the phone first or offer you a consultation to talk over the different approaches and ways they can help you. It is important to have a good rapport with your therapist. You will know early on if they are a right fit for you. Don't just go with the first one. Do some research. Look at results and feedback for a good indication of a therapist's success rate. If private therapy isn't an option for you, then talk with your local G.P and ask about therapies open to you via them.

11

It's Your Life, So Live It

Don't put off until tomorrow what you can do today. It's now or never. Seize the moment. Live for today. What you waiting for? Sometimes later becomes never.

We have all heard these wonderful sayings. We have been told them a million times. Chances are, we have said them just as often. So why do you keep putting things off? Why do you find excuses to start tomorrow? Why do you never get everything done in life that you have always wanted? Why are you not living in the moment and fulfilling the dreams you have?

Anxiety.

That's been your answer up until now, right? Procrastination. Your thoughts and feelings won't allow it to be any other way. But if you fight hard and long enough and practice beating it, you don't need to worry about procrastinating over change. You can live it.

"Procrastination: the action of delaying or postponing something."

You put off loads of things on a daily basis for one reason or another. Let's see if you can change your outlook and stop being a procrastinator in the battle with anxiety.

You have changed your outlook and the anxiety is getting less and less. It is leaving. One of the biggest fears people have at this point is that they don't have anxiety. Or it's controlled and managed. Now they ask, "What do I do with myself?" Remember back to one of the first questions you asked before you set out on the battle with anxiety. What do I want? Now you go back and examine that answer. This tells you what to do in an anxiety-controlled and free life. You do it differently. You make the changes. You continue to work hard at staying on top. You rise to everyday life and the challenges it brings.

Here I offer my advice to living your life. It's yours now and it is to be enjoyed. These are the things I threw myself into the second anxiety didn't control my life. They are all massive game-changers in general.

Give it everything: You will only get out of something what you put into it. No-one will do the hard work for you. Remember, before any long-term gain or pleasure from your change, there may be some pain and discomfort. This does not last forever. Try and see it this way: for an athlete to become the winner and rejoice in his victory, he has hours of hard, intensive training. He pushes beyond limits and pain barriers to achieve what he currently has. You may have to accept a little bit of pain for long term pleasure and gain. It's not going to kill you. It won't leave you weakened and beyond repair. It's short-term pain for long-term gain. It will disappear in time so long as you keep the end goal in sight. You give this change one hundred percent effort every day. Get up when you stumble. Ignore any negative when it comes. Stay focused on you and you alone.

Don't listen to the doubters: Not everyone will think the same way about your change. Some will see it as a negative and will be only too happy to tell you this. Ask yourself these questions about negative people trying to keep you where you are. Do they feed you? Do they provide for you? Do they look after your sanity and well-being? Do they contribute so greatly in your life that you couldn't manage without them? Have a think about that for a second, and no doubt the majority of answers are 'no'. So why should you care about their opinion on what changes you're making and implementing in your life?

If they are not happy with what you are trying to achieve and implement in your life, then why are they in your life? You are doing this for you, for your family, for your happiness. The only person whose opinion matters right now is yours. Thank them for their concern and then carry on.

Remember the end goal: When you have a bad day, when you're low on motivation, when you think you can't keep focus, when it all seems too much – KEEP GOING. Push yourself harder than you have ever pushed. Drive straight through the discomfort and pain, whether it's emotional or physical. What doesn't kill you makes you stronger. You have weighed everything up with the ecology check and you know in your heart of hearts it is all going to be worth it. The end is in sight. The change will make you bigger, brighter and a happier person. It will give you what you want in life. You will fulfil your dreams and goals. There is no better feeling in the world than gaining that personal achievement when you think it isn't possible. Go on, surprise yourself. Reach for the stars. You might be surprised at the outcome.

Change your lifestyle: You have been so used to keeping away from new people, events and activities, that you keep yourself very much alone. No one seems to get it unless they have had it. Everyone thinks it's all in your mind and that alienates us even more. But you are not the same person now. You are not frightened in case a panic or anxiety attack comes. You know full well that you get to control them now and not vice versa. One of the biggest changes you need to make right now is your entire lifestyle.

True friends will always be around. They will always be there for you and they are still there waiting when you need them. Family are the very same. Love is unconditional and it doesn't go away because you have been lost for a while. It remains. Think about all the people who have supported you and been there when you needed them. The first thing you do in your lifestyle change is announce to the whole world you are back and are ready to face life. An invitation to come round or meet for coffee and let people know how much you value and love them is a great starting point. Without going into too much detail, you can explain that for a while you may have been lost, but that time is gone. Now you are going to be more prominent in their life. If they ever need you then you are always there for them.

What you are doing is taking all the power away from past events and focusing on your future. That involves you telling the people who have supported you that you're back. What about the negative people? The ones who may have mocked or only been your friend or supported you when it suited them? It's time to take that person and do an ecology check. See why they are there and what purpose they serve in your life. You are a different person. You are a strong person. You need and deserve to be surrounded with positivity and goodness. If you have people who constantly remind you of the bad things in life and trigger fear of anxiety by harsh words or actions, then it's time to set them free.

You can't control other peoples' actions: Other people, no matter how well intended they may be, will carry out actions which directly or indirectly effect you. You don't get to control that part. The part you can control is your reaction. Again, with everything that is happening to you or around you, take a step back. Look at the action. Ask yourself what was the purpose and the intention behind it using fact vs. thought as shown previously.

For example, you return to work for the first time after an absence. You walk in and say "Good morning" to the boss. They ignore you and walk past. An emotional response would be, what have I done wrong? Or why are they ignoring me? Have I upset them? That's the old you. You are doing very things differently now. Your new way of thinking and behaving lets you avoid heading straight to the negative. You go straight to fact vs. thought.

As a boss he could have payroll etc. to sort out.

He didn't hear you (think about all the times you haven't heard someone). He might have been focused on other work-related events.

He had a late night and an early morning so isn't fully alert and awake.

He had an argument with family or friends so his mind is preoccupied.

There are hundreds of logical, calm reasons why he didn't return your greeting. Now you get to look at all of them instead of going straight to the negative. The easiest way to put that negativity to bed is to communicate when you see the person again.

"Good morning, hope everything is OK. I said good morning before and you didn't reply."

That simple statement will show your compassion and caring for others. This will give your boss the chance to apologise and explain the reason behind their earlier behaviour.

Do something good at least once a day which no one knows about: We all have an inner being. This part is selfless, with a want and need to help and be a good person. Every day, do one selfless act for others. That will make you feel good about your core qualities. This ensures that you stay on the right side of your spiritual self. So many people are prepared to simply take and never give. Those people will have to answer to their own conscious mind. The time has come for you live a happy, selfless life and give back.

Think about all the times no one could see the battle you were facing on the inside. How you wished someone understood, threw their arms around you and said it would all be OK. But no one did. Be that person with the open arms. Remember your superpowers, here. You have them for a reason. Use these occasions to exercise them. It doesn't need to be a grand 'look at me' gesture. Giving your seat up on public transport. Holding a door open for someone. Saying thank you to someone who's helped you or done the same for you. A random good morning text to friends or family with a smiley today I love you message. This is very powerful. This means so much more than a hollow grand gesture done for show. What you do has to be genuine and from the heart. In turn, the world and universal energy will send it back tenfold.

Fill your calendar: Let's think back to the trigger list. Now is the perfect time to start doing the things which once held you back. The activities which gave you so much anxiety you couldn't even talk. Don't be frightened. You are a different person now. You think differently. You act differently. You have more knowledge and understanding than ever before. If you want to go on a night out with friends, let's put that dream into action and go out. Taking baby steps is what you need to do first. That's OK. Let's start to fill your life with things you want to do. If you have a bucket list, then what's stopping you? Get started.

You're not the same anxious, frightened person you were. You are stronger now. As you change your emotional and mental state, you must also change your physical one. Go to an exercise class. Join yoga, a gym, or a walking club. Do things differently. Do things which fill you with happiness. One common mistake for anxiety sufferers is that they get rid of the anxiety, but keep the old routine. Nothing changes for them. Instead of sitting day in and day out with anxiety, they sit day in and day out without anxiety. The 'without' part is a perfect result, but you need to live a better, fuller life than before. Remember the title of this chapter. Remember why you want the change in the first place. You want to enhance and enrich your life so you can go out and get what you want.

Be consistent, learn from anxiety: Anxiety was very powerful at one stage. We agree on that. Now let's look at one of the key traits which made it so powerful. It never gave up. It was constant every day. It gave one hundred percent to hurting, beating and keeping you down. Let's learn something from it. Let's adopt the same approach to being different and living life. Let's use the same tactics anxiety used to hold us back and keep us down. Consistently push, drive and move forward with life. Don't let up. Consistency is the key to making the change long-lasting and having power over it. You can't have one wobble then throw your hands in the air and say, 'Aw well, that's me back to square one'. Remember the steps in the book, the advice on hand, and the direct, no-nonsense approach. Work at creating your new environment and habitual behaviours the same way anxiety worked at you. Consistently.

Increase your own levels of serotonin: What is serotonin? Low serotonin levels have been linked to depression. Serotonin is an important chemical and neurotransmitter in the human body. It is believed to help regulate mood and social behaviour, appetite and digestion, sleep, memory and sexual desire and function. There may be a link between serotonin and depression and anxiety levels.

That's what the majority of antidepressant pills and SSRI medications do (selective serotonin reuptake inhibitors). These increase the levels of serotonin in your system. However, they do take around six to eight weeks to take effect and some people are averse to taking medication of this sort. You can add to your own serotonin levels by doing the following:

1. **Get physical**: One of the most powerful methods for releasing serotonin is physical exercise at any level. If you can join a gym or fitness class then by all means do

so, if you can't, then try ditching the car for walking. If that's not possible try and do something every day, no matter how small, to release as much serotonin as possible. The recommended amount of steps per day for the average person is ten thousand. This equates to five miles. If you can hit half of that then that's a good starting point to work your way up. Pilates, yoga, any form of wellness and keep fit activity is a great place to start. Not only do you exercise, you get to increase your social circle and meet new people. You make friends who don't know about your past, so you start on an even footing.

2. **Less sugar:** If you have low serotonin, you may have intense cravings for sugar. This is your body's way of trying to increase serotonin. Sugar produces insulin, which helps tryptophan enter your brain. However, too much sugar can eventually cause an addiction, insulin resistance, hypoglycaemia and type 2 diabetes. Instead, satisfy your sweet tooth in a healthy way with fruit and natural sweet treats like honey. You are behaving differently, so why not go all in? Let's try cooking from scratch, preparing your own meals and foods and ditching processed foods and high-sugar foods.

   Have you ever made a pasta sauce from scratch? It tastes so much fresher, cleaner and fulfilling that processed ones. If the family haven't cooked anything with you in the past, get them involved and do things together. That alone releases the feel good factor and you enjoy everything even more because it's made by your own hand. Clean out the pantry and ditch the high-sugar, high-salt food groups. Go clean and fresh. It does much more for you than simply changing your eating habits.

3. **Laughter:** One of the last things you do when you have anxiety is laugh. If you do, it's usually false and to please those around you. You do it to make sure they stop asking questions like, "What's wrong?" or "Are you OK?" for the ten millionth time. This makes everything worse. Then you are forced into that circle of falseness and lies we have spoken about when you lead this double life. There are many options here. One of the

best is a comedy club with different acts every night. It's cheap and you're guaranteed to laugh at one of the acts at least, so it's a good bet for a cheap, fun night out. Also satellite TV has a comedy channel on all packages. Put that on and leave it running in the background. I am not saying this is enforced laughter, but every now and then you will pick up on something and you will smile. Then you catch yourself smiling and it grows bigger. For the first time in a long time, your smile and laughter is genuine.

Box set comedy has so many options. There is someone out there for all tastes. You'll be surprised how very powerful laughter can be.

4. **Wellness:** Wellness is also another amazing method. I have spoken about this and shown you a number of methods to achieve it. The benefits of yoga and meditation are immense. They offer us inner calmness and tranquillity. This feeling is second to none, so practise it. In the comfort of your own home, turn down the lights, put on a gentle music track and sit down. Breathe and relax. Sink down into that whole inner awareness mode I have shown. This is very powerful internally at releasing serotonin and calmness. You deserve calmness in life. You have worked hard to battle through the anxiety. You deserve peace in your inner-self.

5. **Get natural day light:** For some people with anxiety leaving the home environment hasn't been high on the agenda. That needs to change. Studies have shown that receiving twenty minutes of natural sunlight on your body every day can boost your energy level and mood. High intensity light serves as a signal, telling the body to stop producing melatonin and start producing serotonin. Lack of exposure to sunlight is a reason for some forms of depression caused by perpetually low serotonin levels. Spending time outside can help reverse this. In fact, spending time in natural light has been shown to provide the same benefits as anti-depressant medications in improving serotonin levels in the brain.

6. **Sleep at night, rise in the morning:** Part of being anxious doesn't let us switch off. This often leads to late nights and irregular sleeping patterns. Now you will sleep at night and be active in the day. Set new patterns. This may take some adjustment and a few late nights. Getting used to going to bed, switching off and not lying awake may take a while. Hit the hay at 10 p.m. or 1 p.m. if possible. When you lie down, breathe, relax and go into the meditative mode we spoke about. Release and relax every muscle in the body. Prepare properly. Avoid coffee or eating before heading to bed. Don't have the TV on in your bedroom. If needed, read a few chapters of a book. No social media. Read a book which holds your focus and attention. Keep learning and keep focusing.

7. **Goodbye social media:** Social media is fine for keeping in touch with friends or family who aren't on the phone or too far away to check up on. But a lot of social media has turned into a place for sales, bullying and falseness. You get to see some inspiring posts and articles but they can be found elsewhere on the net just as easily. You are living a new life. Until you get used to it and become as strong as you need to be, why don't you suspend your social media accounts: Facebook, Twitter, Instagram, Snapchat, Vine, etc.?

   You need to focus on your issues and development, not the world around you. You don't need to see the crazy comments of someone who never had anxiety talking nonsense about it. Or the person who sees it as a weakness. Or any of the other problems social media brings. So, just for now, suspend them and focus on you, your journey, your healing and your strength. You will know when it's time to re-activate them. You will not die without social media. In fact, you will be surprised at how good you feel without it for a while. Remember you are doing things differently. This stage is about setting new patterns, behaviours and emotional stability. What is more important to you? Setting those patterns or a post on social media?

8. **Massage:** Several studies have demonstrated the benefits of massage in boosting serotonin. Massages are effective in reducing cortisol, the stress hormone which blocks production of serotonin. When cortisol is inhibited, the brain is in an optimal state to produce serotonin. Massage therapy can also increase the production of the "reward pleasure" brain chemical known as dopamine.

9. **The power of meditation:** There are numerous forms of meditation, and each one helps increase production of serotonin in the brain. Similar to massage therapy, meditation reduces the levels of cortisol in the brain and invokes a relaxation response. Lower stress levels allow for an increase in serotonin and provide an instant mood-boost.

10. **Familiarity is your friend:** You already know that doing things repeatedly sets up habits and patterns. You already know that you are changing and doing things differently. So let's get familiar with your new patterns and habitual behaviours. Make yourself a schedule. You don't even need to write it down, you can have it in your head if you know it off by heart. Keep to the same routine every morning. Wake at the same time every day and go from there. I will give you an example of a typical day for me when I first made the change. I do the same every day now. I don't question it, because I know it works for me.

06:30: Rise. The first thing I do is I stand in front of my mirror, smile, say good morning and remind myself that no matter what the day throws at me I am going to give it everything I have.

06:30-07:00: Affirmations. I write down my affirmation for the day twenty-five times. I keep it in the present time, not future or past. I pick up my writing pad, look myself in the eye and read them out loud twenty-five times. I always notice how strong and empowered I feel by the end.

07:00-07:30: I shower and get ready for the day ahead. I was always told that if you look the part you will feel the part. If I am working at the practice I will wear my suit and tie. If it's the weekend, I will wear a shirt with a collar and a jersey with it. I always want to look my best. This makes me feel as if I have achieved something every day, even before I leave my home. Making an effort to dress smartly is an achievement for someone who spent ten years not wanting to get out of bed, shower or shave on a daily basis. It makes me proud of how far I have come.

07:30-08:00: Fuel up for the day with a good solid protein breakfast. Again, it is important to eat clean and have a healthy lifestyle. There is no point having a healthy mind if your body is dragging you backwards. All those heavy sugars and sweeteners and too many carbs just make you feel heavy, bloated and sluggish. I have fought so hard to be the person I am. I want to be as sharp as I can every day.

08:00-08:30: Make sure the family are ready for the day. My daughters are fourteen and sixteen. If I don't make sure they are on point, they will go without breakfast, forget something for school, or just take forever and a day to get organised.

09:00: Arrive at the practice. I don't start client sessions until 10:00, so I use my first hour to prepare client info for the day, and light candles and incense burners. Then I spend thirty minutes sitting in my office relaxed and visualising. I run through how I am going to help people that day. I always look at how I can improve what I do to ensure that my clients get the maximum to take away from their session. I sit and prepare my mind for my work. On weekends, I will stay in and do some writing. Or I might create a post. I keep my mind active by relaxation, slowing down after the week and looking forward to spending time with friends or family.

09:00-20:00: In the practice.

20:00-23:00: When I go home I check the kids and see how they got on at school. I catch up on their school work. I sort out any leftover administration and start to close down around 22:00 hrs. Affirmations, again, written down then spoken out loud twenty-five times and then hit the hay. I enter into the breathing cycle I spoke about, slowing everything down to have a good night's rest.

That's not set in stone, but that's what I aim for. At times life takes its toll and things change regularly. I don't see this as an issue. I understand life is full of twists and turns, ups and downs and I take life on its terms. I remain flexible and enjoy the present moment and time. That's all you have.

The key here is to do things differently. Make new patterns and habitual behaviours, because the last set you had weren't really working out that well for you. Change the behaviour and you change the outcome. This should all be fun and exciting to you. You get to play about with new behaviours and ways of life. Try it and if you enjoyed it, do it again. If you didn't, don't do it again and put it on the 'no' list.

It's all about living your life and making each moment count. You are on the road to being anxiety-free.

12

Conclusion and Final Steps
Keeping up the Momentum

You have been remarkable. I am so proud. You have reached the end of the book. This means many different things and I will list a few. You are as strong as I gave you credit for at the very start of this book. You are ready for that change. You are capable. You now have a list of methods and techniques that you didn't have before. You will have already tried the ones you could while reading the book. You will have time afterwards to try the ones you haven't attempted.

You have discovered a different way of thinking, behaving and determining a positive outcome. You have a lot more knowledge on anxiety than you had previously. You can now keep up the momentum in relation to fighting your anxiety. You never asked for the anxiety to intrude in your life. It turned you into something you never wanted to be. But you did ask for help in beating it. This book will give you the tools to do so. Self-help is always the first port of call. If you are reading this book and books like it, then you have that fight left in you. You have the desire to live a normal life once more.

The key word here is momentum. Continue to push past any short-term pain and keep the long-term gain in sight. You need to have an end state. A goal or dream to work towards. When you have that, it makes fighting and moving forward so much easier.

Goal setting: HUGGS. Huge Unbelievably Great Goals. These are long-term. They could take three to five years. They can be anything you really want which can't happen instantly. Things which happen instantly are short-term goals. To achieve your long-term goals, you have to hit the short term goals first to reach that stage. A bit like stepping stones on a journey to an island. Having goals is key to your direction. Otherwise, what's it all for? What's the point in getting anxiety-free if you only sit in a room day in and day out? The goals are the lights in a dark room guiding you to the final destination. That great big, old HUGG.

Always remember you are enough: Stop being so harsh on yourself. For the love of God, stop it. There are plenty of other people who will be harsh, cold, calculating, obtuse and hurtful to us. You don't need to add to that list. You were born unique in every way, shape and form. Being different or having different experiences in life is what makes you who you are. Instead of shame, have pride in it. Love yourself every day.

You were put on this earth for a reason: Don't question the universe, it will answer when the time is right. For now, know that you have been put on this earth for a reason. Everything that has gone before you has happened in the same way. It doesn't matter if you can't see that reason right now. You will one day and all of this will make perfect sense. Instead of thinking, 'Why has this happened to me?' think, 'This is a harsh but powerful learning opportunity. If my children or loved ones suffer, I will be able to relate, help and guide them to the other end. I suffered longer because I had the strength to do that. They won't have to because I have the strength to help them. That's why this happened to me.'

Anxiety has a funny way of sobering your thoughts and outlook on life. It can define your existence in the world or it can make you the person you are destined to be. With millions of sufferers in the country, there are many different treatments for anxiety and phobias. Each has merit in its own right. It is also important to note that one method doesn't fit all. We are all different. But that doesn't mean you shouldn't try every method until you find the one that suits you best.

Never give up or give in.

Channel the inner fight which brought you to this book in the first place. Use that to start every day. If anxiety ever gets too much and your thoughts take you to dark areas of your mind, promise me that you will reach out before any action is taken. I have listed a number of organisations and charities with helplines and numbers at the back of the book. Talk to whoever is listening. Friends, family, GP, help lines, therapists. Anyone is better than no one. I lost my brother to mental health ten years ago and still feel the after-effects around that choice.

You are on the up and up. You will continue to grow in strength every day, until you no longer think about tapping, playing with visions, sounds or feelings. In a few days, weeks or even a month from now, you will stop dead and think, 'Wow – I haven't had one twinge of anxiety today.' And before you know it, you will be going about your day happy as you like, living life on your terms.

Finally, I would like to thank you for buying this book, reading it, and giving it everything you have. This is the end for you reading the book. But it is the beginning for you starting an anxiety-free life. Life is for living. Everything that happens and every choice you make can be turned into a positive. We will finish this book with a simple story.

A farmer owns a horse, and the horse breaks free and runs away. "Bad luck, that is," the neighbour tells him.

"Maybe," the farmer says.

The next day the horse returns with another horse. "Wonderful news," the neighbour tells him.

"Maybe," the farmer says.

The farmer's son takes the new horse out but is thrown and breaks his leg.

"Bad luck," the neighbour says.

"Maybe," the farmer says.

The next day the military draft all young men except the farmer's son.

"Wonderful," the neighbour says.

"Maybe," the farmer says.

You never know what your choices will bring. All you can do is trust that you are the smartest, most thoughtful person making them. Everything happens for a reason. What seems to be a negative event can turn out to be the biggest gift you will ever receive.

God bless each and every one of you on your battle with anxiety.

But remember, you are way more powerful than this emotion will ever be.

13
A Case Study Using the Methods Behind the Book

"I wanted the old, happy KW back, the one I have all the fond memories of; the one I seem to have lost along the way."

KW is a middle-aged male who runs a successful catering business in South West Scotland. He has suffered for years with the stress and strain of life and the crippling anxiety it brought. This lead to severe social anxiety and general anxiety in his day to day life. KW decided to try a different route, having tried most conventional methods and therapies to deal with his anxiety. Here KW gives his views and opinions on the treatment and shares the progress he made using the methods I have shown you in this book.

KW: Initially, I was apprehensive. You see all these TV shows with hypnotists on them, but Kevin was completely different. I felt relaxed and at ease almost instantly and kind of knew straight away this was a good fit for me. The first step is like diving off a 10-metre board at the pool. You have to trust the person guiding you that it's safe and the right option. Once you have made the initial leap by contacting them and having the first meeting, well, I honestly didn't give it a second thought.

I have suffered with stress and anxiety for around three years, with it increasing and getting worse as each day passed. As soon as I woke, I was filled with dread and fear. That heavy unsettling feeling would be most prominent in the morning. Every time I had a thought or an idea that made it worse. It limited me in so many other areas and the biggest part was my motivation and determination to succeed. I tried all the self-talk and self-motivation posts on social media. I understood them, but just didn't have it in me at the time to follow them or act on them. I started to stay indoors a lot more, and eventfully distanced myself more than I should have at the time.

It kind of isolated me and it was a very lonely time, to be honest. It feels like you are the only one suffering and no one else understands. Tough love makes it worse and people saying things like: "It's all in your head" or "You're imagining it" or "Come on, just get up and get on with it" didn't help. At times, it made it all the worse, because I couldn't be like them and just get up and get on with it. It affected my relationships with my friends and family. Even work was starting to suffer because I wouldn't put myself out there for fear of being shot down, told I wasn't good enough or even judged on my appearance. Everything I thought about just seemed to spiral. I could look at a small problem and see it as immense.

I went to my GP, but felt that all he wanted was to treat the symptoms and not the source. He put me on anti-anxiety medication. Looking back, the medication didn't fix the problem. It masked the problem. I was aware that the second I wanted to stop the medication, the problems would re-appear. I have never been one to be dependent on any form of medication and I didn't like the lack of control over my choices, thoughts and feelings which it provided.

Having heard about NLP in the past I decided to look it up and read a bit more. It made perfect sense, so I arranged a session with Kevin and it went from there.

Remarks: When KW first walked into my office, he appeared extremely nervous and shy about his position and situation. During the first half of the session it became apparent that KW was a warm and caring person. He was displaying severe social anxiety and, in certain circumstances, general anxiety, especially when alone with his thoughts at night. He had gotten himself into a typical anxious behavioural pattern. He had a self-destructive internal dialogue which wouldn't allow any positive thoughts, feelings or emotions to be shown to himself by himself.

KW has a fear of speaking with customers and potential new clients for his business. This was hampering the company progress and limiting it to only small-scale events with clients he already knew; or family and friends at weekends. He was turning something he enjoyed and had passion for into an emotional trigger for the anxiety. KW was isolating himself from people and situations which would enhance not only his personal life but his business life, also.

Session 1: The first thing I did with KW was to teach him blockers for his panic and anxiety when the attacks came. We spent the second half of the first session teaching and practising 'calm anchoring' and 'stop not today' from chapter 3.

KW: After the very first session, I left the room on a high. For the first time, I knew I could limit the damage and the control anxiety had over me. Tapping was relentless for the first few days for me and having got my calm anchor during the first session, it was already in place. All I had to do was press the button. I would switch between methods depending on where I was or what I was doing. I preferred tapping in the comfort of my own home and not in public or in company, but I could press my anchor no matter where or when. It would level me and take me to the place I felt calmest in my life.

It was almost like a reset button all of its very own.

Eventually it just became less and less, as the anxiety seemed to actually listen to these two methods. After a few days, it disappeared as soon as I started the blockers. It was as if it knew I was fighting back and it couldn't be bothered to make the effort.

Session 2: When KW returned for his second session, he appeared much calmer and more at peace, although the anxiety was still present. The thought of being put in a position to deal with new clients or people was still a very uncomfortable one. But the lightness he felt, having stopped several panic and anxiety attacks from happening, was a relief. This gave him even more hope and determination. KW is a very kinaesthetic orientated person and that played a part in the second session. Here we used parts integration. This was a deal breaker. The change was immediate for him. It is something to behold when you see that all important shift take place. It can only be described as the same person swapping over to the person they always wanted to be, from the one they didn't. It is always a complete privilege and honour to witness such a shift. It is a thing of beauty.

KW: The second session changed my entire life and that of my friends, family and everyone who supported me. I found it strange when my hands started moving all on their own and I had no control over them. But I followed the instruction and just focused on my breathing. So, I honestly couldn't tell you what happened, but I do remember Kevin saying, "… And now, very gently, open your eyes…" and wow, it was if my eyes were replaced with brand new ones. I could see clearly. The fog that clouded my eyes wasn't present. The constant turning and heaviness in my chest and stomach had left. I felt light, giddy almost and just remember thinking; no way did he just take the anxiety from me.

I remember looking for it and trying to feel for it where it always sat. But all I felt was lightness. I am not sure that even makes sense, but that's what I felt. Light and very different. Kevin asked me, if I was standing in a room now with ten new clients and had to give a sales pitch on my business, how would I react? "Bring it on" was my answer. This was so surreal that surely it wouldn't be real.

But it was real, and it was instant. A few days later, I secured a massive catering contract in central Scotland. Before Kevin, I probably wouldn't even have attended the meeting. I managed to walk into a meeting with a lot of pressure on me to get it right, sell myself, sell my business and secure a new contract for the company. And I did. I totally did and I nailed it. I think the pride I felt in myself that day was something I will remember for the rest of my life. It was a defining moment for me.

Session 3: KW arrived excited and full of the joys of spring. He hadn't had a panic or anxiety attack in a week. He still had little twinges here and there, but they came and went extremely fast, now. They weren't enough to bother or affect him. He was hitting the gym every day and walking his dog for longer periods of time. He was starting to live his life to the full. The small twinges of anxiety were still twinges and I wanted to teach him how to deal with them. This session focused on his internal dialogue. Words = thoughts = emotions. I used a reframe and sub modalities to deal with the residue of the anxious behaviours.

I used kinaesthetic methods on the sub modalities as KW was predominantly kinaesthetic in his emotions and feelings. He didn't have any pictures or sounds to go with them. His body language and words showed that very early on. He used statements like, 'I feel', 'this feeling', pointing to his chest area when explaining how anxiety manifested itself in him. The good thing about these sessions was that we took the heavy predominate anxious feeling away. This gave him a desire and hunger to learn, do more, and push himself to the limits in this battle.

We were getting very close to the end, with only one more session left after this one. Yes, that's correct. Four sessions in total is all that's needed to be different. Four sessions and four different methods culminating in a whole new you. That's the plan and the agenda I run off. Some people may try and get you to take them up on eight to twelve sessions for anxiety therapy. But if it's done in this direct, effective way, four is all you need.

KW: I have to say, it felt a little strange when Kevin asked me to bring up what was left of my anxiety and really feel it. I hadn't given it much notice for the past week, after the second session. But I put all my trust in his methods and we brought it up on a scale of about 8 I think at the time. One sentence made all the difference in this session. He told me that anything you can do with an object you have in your hand, you can do with an object or feeling inside you.

I had so much fun putting frames around the feeling, pausing it, changing its colour and pushing it into the distance. It felt so very real and, at the same time, slightly sad that this thing I have carried for so long was leaving me. I guess a little bit of shock and panic set in. Now I have to actually live my life just as I promised myself if I ever got anxiety free. That was short-lived. I was then shown and taught about my internal dialogue. How every word triggered a thought, then the thought leads onto a feeling and the feeling guided my actions. If I became more aware, I could change them at the very first stage. Every morning, that's exactly what I did. I got up, headed straight to the gym and then took my dog for a walk. It's amazing to see how this all started with a word. But it did, and now I am in control. I get to choose the word. And I choose happiness.

Session 4: As KW arrived, I have to admit I was filled with pride. His anxiety was gone. He had spoken with his doctor to ask him to drop and eventually remove the anti-anxiety medication. KW was now on the bare minimum. He had another review in a week to stop it, should he continue his remarkable journey? This session is based on current and future planning. Actions. Talking about and showing him how to behave and the different life style choices he has open to him. I also used hypnotherapy and increased his confidence, drive and determination. We rocket it up to the stars. We culminate all the sessions in this one. We test his own internal dialogue. I asked Kevin what he wanted now and his reply was simple. "To get back out there and take the world and everything in it, and use it to my advantage."

KW: Session 4 was a perfect end for me. Although I still wasn't sure what I would do being completely anxiety-free, and how I should approach life. My confidence was sky high by the time Kevin finished with me. I identified that my internal dialogue was damaging and made the choice to change it. My excitement for life and my business was back. I honestly didn't think it was possible in a really short period of time. I have gone from being virtually a recluse, to pushing my business beyond what I thought possible, and feeling happy and content in myself. I am proud of who I am and what I achieved.

I am finally me again. I love me and I love it.

Remarks: Kevin's case was typical of modern day anxiety. You get yourself flustered, you react badly to other people's actions, and then you worry about the future. Because you can't see it, anxiety comes along and just makes everything ten times worse. KW was put on an anxiety therapy which was designed to eliminate and remove anxiety quickly and effectively. For everyone who doesn't believe in a quick fix, four sessions for something that you have lived with for years is quick and extremely effective.

Closing comments – KW: I never once thought, at the start, that these simple methods and techniques would take me from 0 to 100 in such a short space of time. My anxiety is gone. My medication for anxiety is gone. My confidence and self-esteem are sky high. I am living and pushing my dreams every single day. I love how my life has changed, If anxiety ever does try to make an appearance, not only am I cured, I also have all the tools myself now to deal with it. But I am way too strong for anxiety. I truly believe it won't be back any time soon.

Kevin: A few months have passed since I last saw KW and in that time he has gone from strength to strength. He is living a life he wants, and arranging lots of meetings and business opportunities to tell the world about his business. He is continuing his pursuit of fitness and remains a very nice and calm man.

Case Number

"I just wish this negative devil on my shoulder would shut up and allow me to live my life and not fill my head with negativity, overthinking and dread."

Ms D is a female in her late fifties. She struggles with overthinking and the anxiety it brings her in relation to the future and what is going on in her life. She has been married for over twenty-five years and has one adult child who now has moved on with her own life. This has created a vacuum in Ms D life. With anxiety playing a major role, she has no direction on how to fill this. A complete shift in the family dynamics has compiled the anxiety to levels where she struggles to find any joy in her current situation. Ms D is adamant that medication is not the way forward. Having read previous case studies on the results and impact, she is prepared to try NLP and hypnotherapy.

Ms D: I am tired of feeling no joy or having any motivation to do anything. For example, Christmas is around the corner and I haven't even put a tree up. I haven't decorated or done any real preparation for it. I haven't even acknowledged that it is coming. Christmas is a time for joy and family but I just feel empty toward it. All I do is overthink and that makes the anxiety even worse. I just wish this negative devil – as I call it – on my shoulder would shut up and allow me to live my life and not fill my head with negativity, overthinking and dread. I have seen lots of different adverts on NLP on social media. I have done some research. I have a background in Pilates – I used to teach it. I know the importance of inner wellness and positive thinking. I just can't seem to get my own mind to budge.

Remarks: Ms D entered my practice and I knew from the early stages that this would be a powerful, fast shift for her. She was gentle, genuine and I could see the pain etched on her face. She knew what needed to happen. She just couldn't do it herself. She fully understood that she could beat this anxiety but she didn't know how. It was very clear that Ms D was very audio-orientated when it came to her predominate learning system. Our focus would use that to remove and replace the negativity with a different behaviour. This would allow her to lose her anxiety and live the life she once lived.

Session 1: This was based all around her negative internal dialogue. Words = thoughts = emotions. Ms D was in a typical anxious pattern of self-talk. We had to change that. I used an example to show her just how effective words can be on changing your thoughts and feelings. If the thought is positive then the voice that goes with it is positive also. At this stage, I used sub modalities audio, showing her how to listen to the voice and then turn the volume all the way down to mute. Then we looked at any residual anxiety and used tweaking and teaching her how to change the feelings kinaesthetically.

Ms D: Straight away everything felt very different. Usually that negative voice eats away at me all day. Now it seems quiet, allowing only the positive voice to talk to me in my mind. I searched for it and listened really carefully but it wasn't there anymore. This changed my entire life. I felt different. I felt light and fresh. The first thing I did that weekend was to go out and buy a Christmas tree. I decorated it and invited my daughter and granddaughter over. It felt amazing.

Session 2: This session revolved around parts integration at a subconscious level to replace the anxious behaviour. This was a massive game changer for Ms D. For the first time in a long time, we removed all her anxiety. This let her move forward carefree and in control.

Ms D: Blinking hell. I have no way of describing what happened with my hands and my thoughts but I feel one hundred percent different. I feel happy. I feel free. I feel like nothing can stop me, now. I will just wake every day, smile, and go about my business. I feel like a whole new person. I get to control all my words, thoughts and emotions not the other way around. It feels amazing.

This particular client recovered and became anxiety free after only two sessions. The third and fourth sessions were spent confidence-building and reaction adjustment. We focussed on how only you can control your reactions to the incidents, situations and problems you face. If you go into a day with a good outlook, a good heart and great intentions, the day is going to deliver exactly what you make it deliver. This result was very special to me. It has allowed this person to wake and go at every day now with all the energy in the world behind her.

Closing comments: Ms D. If someone told me a few weeks back that after such a small period of time I would be anxiety-free, I would have laughed at them. But that's exactly what I am now. I have a greater understanding of the mind, both consciously and subconsciously. I know how powerful my own words can be. I am honestly looking forward to the future and all it may bring. I feel very strong. Very strong indeed.

Kevin: Ms D was very audio-representational and the biggest damaging factor was the voice with negativity. What's the best way to deal with an annoying noise? You turn the volume down. That proved a game changer for this lady. The parts integration ensured that the voice didn't have a platform. It was simply an anxious behaviour and we removed the behaviour. I am still in contact with Ms D. She is extremely busy living life and helping plan her daughter's wedding. Still full of fun, life and energy. A truly remarkable lady.

References

1. *Modelling with NLP* by Robert Brian Dilts, 2017, Dilts Strategy Group
2. *NLP Workbook: A Practical Guide to Achieving the Results You Want* by Joseph O'Conner, 2001, Thorsons.
3. *NLP: How to Use Neuro-Linguistic Programming to Change Your Life* by Ali Campbell, 2015, Hay House.
4. *The Anxiety and Phobia Workbook* by Edmund J Bourne, 1 Mar 2015, New Harbinger Publications
5. *Tapping the Healer Within: Using Thought-field Therapy to Instantly Conquer Your Fears, Anxieties, and Emotional Distress* by Roger J Callahan & Richard Turbo, 2001, McGraw Hill Education

Resources
Books

1. *NLP: How to Use Neuro-Linguistic Programming to Change Your Life* by Ali Campbell, 2015, Hay House.
2. *Tapping the Healer Within: Using Thought-field Therapy to Instantly Conquer Your Fears, Anxieties, and Emotional Distress* by Roger J Callahan & Richard Turbo, 2001, McGraw Hill Education.
3. *NLP Workbook: A Practical Guide to Achieving the Results You Want* by Joseph O'Conner, 2001, Thorsons.
4. *The Anxiety and Phobia Workbook* by Edmund J Bourne, 1 Mar 2015, New Harbinger Publications.
5. *Change Your Life in 7 Days* by Paul McKenna, 2010, Sterling.
6. *Just Get On With It! A Caring, Compassionate Kick Up the Ass!* by Ali Campbell, 2010, Hay House.
7. *The Structure of Magic, Vol. 1: A Book About Language and Therapy* by Richard Bandler and John Grinder, 1975, Science and Behavior Books.
8. *The Structure of Magic, Vol. 2: A Book About Language and Therapy* by Richard Bandler and John Grinder, 1976, Science and Behavior Books.
9. *Trance-Formations: Neuro-Linguistic Programming and the Structure of Hypnosis* by Richard Bandler and John Grinder, 1981, Real People Press.
10. *Patterns of the Hypnotic Techniques of Milton H Erickson, MD Vol. 1* by Richard Bandler and John Grinder, 1975, Meta Publications.

Websites

www.serenitynlp.com – Here you can find resources to all the different methods and bookings with Kevin Mullin.

www.richardbandler.com – The main web page for the co-creator of NLP and access to his personal page.

www.purenlp.com – for NLP training worldwide.

Jargon Buster

NLP: Neuro Linguistics Programming.
EFT: Emotional Freedom Technique (Tapping).
EMDR: Eye Movement Desensitisation and Reprocessing.
CBT: Cognitive Behaviour therapy.
LEM: Lateral Eye Movements. Tapping: Another name for TFT/EFT

Serotonin: A compound present in blood platelets and serum, which constricts the blood vessels and acts as a neurotransmitter.

Havening: A healing modality designed to help individuals overcome problems which are the consequence of traumatic encoding. The Havening techniques belong to a larger group of methods called psych sensory therapies. These use sensory input to alter thought, mood and behaviour.

Reiki: Reiki is a form of alternative medicine developed in 1922 by Japanese Buddhist Mikao Usui. Since originating in Japan, reiki has been adapted into varying cultural traditions across the world.

Placebo: A medicine or procedure prescribed for the psychological benefit to the patient rather than for any physiological effect.

Dopamine: A compound present in the body as a neurotransmitter and a precursor of other substances including adrenaline.

Hormone: A hormone is any member of a class of signalling molecules produced by glands in multicellular organisms. These are transported by the circulatory system to target distant organs, regulating physiology and behaviour.

Rfn: Rifleman. The rank given to private soldiers enlisting in to the Light Division of the British Army.

GPMG: General Purpose Machine Gun weapon system.

Bn: Battalion is the name given to a regiment of the British Army.

Jock: A nickname used by non-Scottish people used to describe a Scottish national.

Sub modalities: The fine distinctions or the subsets of the Modalities (Visual, Auditory, Kinaesthetic, Olfactory, Gustatory, and Ad). These are part of each representational system which encode and give meaning to our experiences.

Reframe: NLP Reframe & NLP Reframing. In NLP, a reframe is changing the meaning of a communication by changing the context, the frame size or other changes that put the communication into a situation where the meaning is altered.

Parts Integration: The NLP technique for internal conflict resolution. The NLP Parts Integration technique creates harmony between parts of the unconscious mind so that their values are in alignment. A person with 'Integrated Parts' is congruent, empowered and clear in their decisions and actions.

Visualisation: The representation of an object, situation, or set of information as a chart or another image.

Chakra: The Sanskrit word Chakra literally translates to wheel or disk. In yoga, meditation, and Ayurveda, this term refers to wheels of energy throughout the body.

G.P.: General Practitioner is a term used for a local doctor in the UK.

Recommended Reading

1. *Just Get On With It! A Caring, Compassionate Kick Up the Ass* by Ali Campbell, 2010, Hay House.
2. *NLP: How to Use Neuro-Linguistic Programming to Change Your Life* by Ali Campbell, 2015, Hay House.
3. *Awaken The Giant Within: How to Take Immediate Control of Your Mental, Emotional, Physical and Financial Destiny!* by Anthony Robbins, 2001, Simon and Schuster.
4. *Notes from a Friend* by Anthony Robbins, 2001, Simon and Schuster.
5. *Mindfulness: How to Live Well by Paying Attention* by Ed Halliwell, 2015, Hay House.
6. *NLP Workbook: A Practical Guide to Achieving the Results You Want* by Joseph O'Connor, 2012, Harper Collins.
7. *Mediation: Coming to Know Your Mind* by Matteo Pistono, 2017, Hay House.
8. *The Power of Positive Thinking* by Norman Vincent Peale, 2012, Ebury.